this grief thing FU****NG sucks

TAYA MIKADO

 FriesenPress

One Printers Way
Altona, MB R0G 0B0
Canada

www.friesenpress.com

Copyright © 2022 by Taya Mikado
First Edition — 2022

All rights reserved.

No part of this publication may be reproduced in any form, or by any means, electronic or mechanical, including photocopying, recording, or any information browsing, storage, or retrieval system, without permission in writing from FriesenPress.

ISBN
978-1-03-913819-3 (Hardcover)
978-1-03-913818-6 (Paperback)
978-1-03-913819-3 (eBook)

1. Poetry, Subjects & Themes, Death, Grief & Loss

Distributed to the trade by The Ingram Book Company

Dedicated to my parents, Karen and Don Mikado,
because *with* them,
this book wouldn't have been possible.

Table of Contents

SUMMARY OF EVENTS	VII
PREFACE	IX
BOOK LAYOUT	XV
DISCLAIMER	XVII
MARCH 7	2
YOU ARE RESILIENT	10
WELCOME	16
WHAT WILL IT	23
A WIDOW, A WARRIOR	29
OUR MENTAL HEALTH	34
WHERE DID YOU GO	45
PILLOW	49
IT'S NOT ABOUT WHAT YOU SAY	52
WHERE WE ARE NOW	59
MOTORCYCLE LOVE STORY	63
WELCOME PT.2	68

DEFEATED	72
TRAUMA CALLED	77
TODAY I LEARN, SO TOMORROW WE GROW	81
BIKINI ON A GRAVESTONE	85
"IT'S MEANT TO BE"	93
BED	97
CAN'T HELP BUT THINK OF YOU	101
OH	107
SYMPATHY CARDS	113
WHY ARE YOU PULLING THE RUG?	117
BUT WE ARE ALL JUST THE SAME	123
RED	131
GRIEF, A STORY TO MY PARTNER	134
FIVE YEARS LATER	139
THANK YOU	143
KARENDIPITY	149

TRIGGER WARNINGS

TW // death
TW // suicide
TW // racism

SUMMARY OF EVENTS

Although this book should describe the following situations more elegantly, I hope that this brief summary of events will provide you with my qualifications (if we want to call it that) for writing a book on grief as a young adult.

In August of 1998, I made Karen and Don Mikado's party of two, a party of three. Two years later, my beautiful sister, Sam, made us a party of four. Sam was born just early enough to meet our maternal grandfather. Months after Sam's arrival, this grandfather passed away, yet Mom embraced her role as a mother and grieved with incredible grace while raising us to the best of her abilities. Consequently, grief and heartache were not completely foreign to our family, or to my parents. As time went on, we became more familiar with the unpredictable ways that grief can materialize. In 2011, we tasted new grief when our paternal grandmother had a stroke, leaving her completely unlike the person she was before. And although these experiences are not easy for anyone to face, Sam and I were lucky to have compassionate parents who supported us while helping us build toolkits for future broken hearts.

It was March 7th, 2012, when my dad passed away at forty-seven years old. I was thirteen, in Grade 8, and wholly unaware of what this would bring with it. Mom modelled strength, perseverance, and resilience as she faced headwinds while navigating our family toward happiness. She gave us incredible lives despite the immense despair she continued to feel. She demonstrated the importance of finding time for oneself, to grieve, to hate grief, and to discover different kinds of happiness. The happiness she now sought would have to exist alongside incredible agony, and it would require her to redefine how she saw her life, her pleasures, and her identity.

By embracing new experiences and responding empathetically to them, she gracefully led our small family toward joy and stability, even when it felt impossible to find.

Later, in 2013 and 2014, grief took new forms in our lives as we lost our paternal grandparents and our paternal uncle. Through it all, Mom radiated hope and love, providing me and Sam with resources, support, and answers that helped us to work through sorrows while searching optimistically for the better times ahead.

However, on May 5th, 2017, Mom passed away at forty-five years old. I was eighteen and had just finished my first year of university 1,200 kms from home. Sam was only in Grade 11 and had not yet finished high school, so I moved back home, and we began our journey of caring for ourselves and each other. Alongside grief, we inherited a plethora of responsibilities and independence. Undoubtedly, this grief would be far different from others we'd experienced. Our rock, our cheerleader, the woman who guided us through the fires of grief that came before, wouldn't be here to help. But taking what we had learned and doing what we could to make ourselves happy, we (kind of) navigated away from the fires that burned. Though the fires never seem to go out, and we can always feel their heat, we have found different ways to keep cool and continue enjoying life with our friend grief.

It is these (rather sucky) events that have led to the creation of this book. And it this collection of stories that I hope will help others prepare themselves for grief, loss, and the mental health repercussions that follow. Anyway, thank you for taking the time to read thus far, and I sincerely hope you enjoy the rest of this book.

PREFACE

In all honesty, writing this book was not something I ever imagined I would do. Or any book for that matter. I admit I'm not a great writer, and I have little experience publicly sharing my emotions and feelings. Years ago, I would have thought it was a joke that I would eventually write about grief. Frankly, it still seems like a joke. And it doesn't help that some days I can't help but cringe or become slightly nauseous when reading through what I have written (maybe it's just that bad ... you've been warned). But it's on the days that I find myself bawling into a pillow or screaming spiritedly in my car that reading and writing make their way to the forefront of my life. Writing has allowed me to express unwanted emotion and leave it on the page, while reading has taught me that my feelings are normal and that they are valid. And as many grievers know, we have some wicked memory lapses after a difficult loss, so without all the things I'd written, I don't think I would be able to remember my thoughts and feelings (good and bad) as astutely. Undoubtedly, reading and writing have been tools to befriend grief. Though I may not always love my writing, it's been worth it for the days that grief leads me astray.

That being said, writing was actually an enterprise that my mom was hoping to tackle after facing many of her own unique experiences with grief. Maybe, subconsciously, this book is my attempt to bring her dream to life. And although I believe she would have written this much more eloquently, I think many similar thoughts would have been highlighted.

As you will come to understand in the rest of this section, convincing myself to publish this for others to read required a lot of thought. Originally, ***This Grief Thing F**KING Sucks*** was my attempt to make sense of life, death, and grief ... for my eyes only. Once I saw the volume of notes, poems, and stories that I'd written, I decided that it wouldn't be the worst idea to try to organize them into one place that I could revisit from time to time. However, I never thought that I would be confident enough to share them with others. Even though for a long time, I wanted to be able to talk about it more, to talk about how I miss Mom and Dad, and to ask my friends how grief has affected them, for a multitude of reasons, I've been scared to. Despite my lack of confidence and my abundance of fears, I knew that I would need to take the first step to begin these conversations, and really, this book has become that first step. Knowing firsthand that there are a lot of nuances in conversations about grief, I thought that one way to begin conversations comfortably for everyone is by sharing my own perspectives. So, that's sort of how *This Grief Thing F**KING Sucks came about,* the long and winding process of turning my experiences with grief into a book. Though I am still not totally confident that what I have to say will be meaningful to others, I hope that it can at least spark healthy conversations and provide some light to shadowed areas of grief. I am also hoping that those who are preparing themselves for grief, those confused by the illusions of grief, or those who might want to hear that they are not alone with their feelings can find something they want to hear in this book. Ultimately, my wish is that this book will impact the world with even a morsel of positivity, and maybe illuminate some of the beautiful effects and moments that go unnoticed amidst the ugly (a whole lot of ugly).

    I have now said a lot of different things about my intentions for this book, and so on, but what is this book really about? What a great question. I really don't know. Simply, I think that I have written about a variety of topics, but I am going to leave what I've written up to the interpretation of your divine minds and unique experiences, since I cannot guarantee that you will leave with the same conclusions that I have attempted to detail.

So, does telling you that this book can be about everything, and anything, suffice as an answer? All jokes aside, these intros are my attempts to clarify some thoughts about this piece that may help guide your reading, but I believe that ultimately, this book, and what you take away from it, depends on how you experience and interact with it (far beyond what I've narrated).

So, what is grief? Simply and explanatorily, I understand it as the natural response to loss. But, due to the subjective nature of what makes up our natural response, I cannot provide you with an exact definition that would allow you to spot grief in yourself or in those around you. Rather, "grief" can encompass an array of responses—physical and emotional—dependent on the person and dependent on what has been lost. And grief, like most experiences, becomes a part of who are by contributing to how we act, how we feel, and how we perceive the world. Consequently, grief it is not something that we just "get over." The false impression that we can stop grieving tends to arise when the idea of grief is thought of as being synonymous with specific emotions like longing, mourning, or sadness. But just because those emotions are absent momentarily does not mean that someone has stopped grieving. It is clear to me that I am still grieving even when certain traditionally understood grief emotions are not present. There still exists a low hanging cloud shadowing the joy that I feel after I've lost someone I love, as though it changes the atmospheric pressure such that the joy also feels . . . bitter? And even years later, the cloud still exists, affecting my emotions and thoughts in ways that surprise me. So, grief is not just the presence or absence of specific emotions after a loss. Rather, grief seems unpredictable, existing beyond temporal constraints, as though it walks between the synapses of emotion and personality, of character and feelings, all while dancing through our memories. And I often forget how deeply grief influences and changes how I think and what I do. Much like trauma (which is often an unwanted accessory to grief), grief tattoos itself onto who we are, continuing to shape who we become. This is why grief exists as a part of us long after the loss, and this is why grief does not just go away. However, confusion can arise when we say that we have, in the past tense, grieved. But just because we have grieved does not mean that we are not still grieving or that we won't later grieve. So, it seems like there are almost endless amounts of grief to be grieved, and sometimes it sure feels that way. Nonetheless, I have no doubt that we all grieve, and it is likely we all will continue to grieve; but maybe griefs' lingering company is (somewhat) welcome when we begin to find its hidden beauties.

If this theory of grief doesn't really add up, it may be best to try and understand grief by identifying what grief is not. Grief is not a mental illness, though it may be a catalyst for different forms of mental instability. Grief is not uniform, because everyone is a product of different experiences and genes leading to unique responses. Grief is not just emotions; it's also our physical responses to loss, like the stress and adrenaline that riddles our nervous systems when we are hurting or shocked. And grief is not just a passerby; rather, it becomes a part of who we are by continuing to influence our thoughts and choices long after the loss (maybe better described as a parasite, lol).

All that being said, it seems that language is wholly limited in how it can describe and detail what we mean by grief. Though I have attempted to explain it, I am quite unsatisfied with the explanations. They all feel unable to capture the multitude of feelings that grief elicits and all the many ways that it continues to materialize. I find it haunting that no combination of words adequately characterizes the essence of what it is, and what it does. And although it seems incomprehensible, like something you can't quite paint a picture of, we all experience and live with it. Grief. Jeez ... I guess that is what this book is about, the mysterious phenomenon that is grief.

~

Now, before we begin, I need to clarify that I have written this book in honour of, and to honour, my amazing parents who have left me with many lessons and laughs about grief. I hope that the beautiful memories of these two people will continue to bring joy to those who knew them and now to those learning about them. I also want to acknowledge and emphasize that without my incredible sister, the creation of this book would not have been possible. Sam has taught me so much about grief, and she has been there to help me in every battle against it. It is because of her tremendous support and wonderful humour that I am able to share my experiences and laugh at them. Without Sam, I wouldn't have had the confidence to publish this book and I wouldn't have had the support to grieve as I needed; for it all and more, I am beyond grateful for you Sam (Also, I love you—I can't forget to say that!). I will also add that the kindness and empathy that has been extended to me by so many people has been incredibly important to my journey with grief and to understanding the ways in which individuals and communities colour my life. By writing this book, I hope to give back to the world some of the help and happiness that these people and communities have provided me.

Finally, I want to acknowledge a few of the many privileges that have allowed me to write this book. Without the assurance from my mom that any form of grief was normal, I wouldn't have had the confidence to write openly about my relationship with grief. Without having my basic needs met, I wouldn't have had the option to spend time thinking about grief and mental health. Without learning that sharing our emotions is important for growth and happiness, I wouldn't have been able to notice and address where grief was hurting me. Without access to various mental health resources, I would never have begun to work through the trauma and pain that came with grief, limiting so many of my capabilities. And without the additional strain of numerous barriers that could have presented themselves, I am very grateful to have been afforded the opportunity to sit here today and to write this book.

BOOK LAYOUT

As you have likely detected, the layout of this book is slightly different from some of the more common book styles. When deciding how I wanted to formulate this book, I knew that I wanted to highlight some of the poetry I have written, while also including a discourse about the experiences and thoughts that have influenced how I process and move forward with grief. Accordingly, I decided to follow the poems with descriptions or stories pertaining to them. As a result, you do not have to read this book in any specific order. If you read from cover to cover the poems will align, roughly, with the temporal sequence of events that took place, but that's not necessarily how or when they were written. If you are interested in just the poetry, or the stories, you can also read selectively. Poetry itself is a beautiful medium to learn because you gain what you give, and we may all walk away with different ideas and perspectives. So, there is more to be found in each of these poems than what I subsequently describe, and I hope to hear what you find. I also hope that by creating a book of this nature, you will be able to shape your experience in a way that suits your style of reading, learning, and entertainment. And then, maybe, if we are lucky, you will walk away from this book better prepared for grief or with a greater understanding of how grief affects your life—but to make sure we do that, write in this book, rip out the pages you don't like, do whatever you need to do to it that will help you take what you want from it.

DISCLAIMER

Grief is incredibly subjective. There is no doubt that grief materializes differently for different people and that it can be influenced by nearly anything. Because of this, there is no way that this book will capture what grief is for others, and I hope it doesn't feel like I am trying to do that. Rather, if I present opinions regarding grief, it is to provide greater insight into where my journey has led me.

Additionally, since I am not educated in grief counselling, neurobiology, or psychiatry, these thoughts and opinions are not to be taken as advice! Rather, I hope that sharing my thoughts can be seen as an opportunity to learn another version of grief. I have found comfort in learning the perspectives of others, in knowing that other people feel the same way, and I hope that others can find comfort in them as well. But I may not be the most reliable narrator; and my perspective and thoughts may be fogged by masks of emotion and my own grief, so take what you want, and I hope you love what you leave with. Ultimately, I could be wrong about all the opinions I've shared; I know that, and I want you to know that, but the one thing I know is how I've felt (sort of), so I hope that that can suffice as knowledge for this book. Ooof.

I also want to mention that with this book I am hoping to create safer spaces in the grief community for all of us. By trying to share an honest discourse with you about my grief, I hope that we can work toward normalizing these conversations, empathizing with different forms of grief, and destigmatizing topics like grief, death, and mental health. Due to its nature, the grief community is already a difficult one to be a part of, so hopefully we can stop adding gas to its fires and find more ways embrace the beautiful and the ugly parts of it.

Finally, as it can already be assumed, this book is unorthodox. When I decided to create a piece that would publicly present my perspectives and experiences, I wanted to be candid with the way the information was shared, and I wanted to do so in a way I would love to read. So, I have formatted this information to provide an honest reflection of myself and my experiences with death. To ensure that I am being as honest as I can, I even changed the title of this book from *You Are Resilient*, a statement that has helped me as well as hurt me throughout grief, to This Grief Thing F**KING Sucks because that's actually what I've wanted to title this book. Out of fear that people wouldn't like it, and because I assumed people would want to read something more positive, I stayed away from such a passionate title. But after reflecting on my title choices and what I would have wanted to read when Dad died, I couldn't think of a more attractive phrase to someone freshly introduced to the horrors that accompany grief than This Grief Thing F**KING Sucks. However, as I have mentioned, there is beauty within grief, and this book explores those avenues as well. Unironically, I find that this title also manifests an incredible amount of beauty in the way that it validates hurt and it liberates those people for whom resilience has become an expectation. Anyway, buckle up. I hope you are now adequately prepped for the journey ahead.

MARCH 7

it wasn't an accident
just an accident in his head

everything was an adventure in his world,
contingent on youth
it made sense that he wouldn't grow old

though there is much we will miss,
life with new lenses
will teach us new lessons

even when sentiments of joy
are muted by wounds

and when minds echo the disagreements
everyone takes some blame,
inhaling against the cement walls

but to forgive, or to forget
to take down pictures,
or to put more up

we're just lost and confused,
no one really knows what to do

and last night when you came into my room
told me you loved me—
had you already left?

suddenly it all becomes irrelevant
when good times are all I see

I wish that's how it was days ago,
to have more is in our dreams,
when we share the best moments of our lives with someone
who is suddenly gone

March 7th was the day that Dad died; and just as this book symbolizes my journey to understand grief, so does this poem. It was this day that grief made its unwelcome debut into my life.

As a 13-year-old, who, the day before, had the picture-perfect nuclear family, all I could find myself thinking about was what would be lost because of this. The moments that Sam, Mom, and I would now navigate alone. Who was going to teach me and Sam how to drive? Mom could, but with her driving history—and a three-inch-thick file of speeding tickets—I knew that we would need to diversify our driving education. And there were so many things I was excited to do with Dad, so many things I wanted to do to make him proud. All of this felt lost, the hope, the dreams, and, to an extent, me. It soon became clear that Dad had filled so many niche roles in my life, contributing significantly to who I thought I was and who I wanted to be. Without him, I felt like I had lost a large part of my identity; and many of the doors I thought I'd eventually walk through began to close.

Soon after I'd exhausted myself thinking about what losses would follow Dad, fear crept into my thoughts. I feared people, judgment, and difficult conversations. How would I explain my new familial structure to friends? How could I tackle pernicious opinions about my family? I was scared, confused, and entirely unaware that many of these questions would go unanswered, or without a satisfying answer, for a large part of my journey with grief.

~

I created this poem out of a note that I had typed the day that Dad died. By turning the thoughts and questions I'd jotted down into a poem, I created a method to work through emotions and thoughts that I intentionally tried to stay away from. But by staying away from them, I wasn't evolving into a person who could befriend grief. Not that I needed to, or that I should ignore the pain that it had caused me, but the lack of a relationship with something so close to me left me feeling unsettled. I never felt sure about what I understood of Dad's death and how it had continued to affect me. But by writing a poem from this note, I began to learn and understand. I learned that my original thoughts about Dad's death mattered greatly. They not only illustrated the types of reactions that I have had to trauma and grief, but they illuminated how I began to process Dad's passing. For instance, when I realized that the note was filled with guilt, heartbreak, and fear, it dawned on me that these are some of the feelings I hate most. Now, by knowing that these feelings were an immediate response to hearing that Dad had died, I understand why I have continued to have such adverse reactions to these feelings in other situations. I never let myself process or accept these feelings. I always felt like I had to battle guilt, heartbreak, and fear to make them go away; so anytime they came back, I would become defensive and prepare to battle. But these fights weren't helping me learn about grief or how to understand these emotions; instead, they left me exhausted and anxious about when they would return. And I still don't know what grief is exactly, but as I have begun to let my guard down and work through how I felt after Dad died, I've become more accepting and empathetic toward myself and these emotions. I see that my guilt and heartbreak emerge from the love I have for Dad and that I wish I could express to him. Though these are really crappy emotions to feel, it's beautiful that they come from a place filled with incredible memories and love for person he was. Clearly there's more to these emotions and more to understand, but by writing this poem my relationship with grief has grown . . . even if getting here has been a hike, and there might not be a peak to this mountain, it's been worth it because I feel healthier and happier with each step of the trek.

So, as I have explained, this poem reflects my thought process when first learning about Dad's death, but it also demonstrates one of the immediate desires I had. As we can see, the poem is sporadic and disorganized, yet it is trying to embody structure and rhythm. The juxtaposition of these forces illustrate the desire for structure that was rooted in my feelings following the traumatic day. I think that it is common for grievers to desire structure. Although the pieces that we try to provide structure to are often inconsistent or incomprehensible, bringing order to chaos can be calming, and it can provide us with much needed stability. Maybe that's what this book really is, an attempt to stabilize my life with grief. However, if this poem teaches me anything, it's that structure gives a moment of rest, but the chaos contained is where I will find belly laughs, heartache, love, and growth.

~

I want to emphasize how important the first line of this poem is to me. The first line of this poem soon became one of the biggest lies and most counterintuitive parts of grief that resulted from my dad's death. After losing Dad, these normally mundane questions became haunting annoyances reviving flutters of grief throughout my body.

> "What does your dad do? Is your dad coming to the game? Where is your dad?"

The first time I heard one of these questions, I stopped dead in my tracks. It felt as though time had stopped as a rush of thoughts began to pulse through my mind. I quickly turned to the first thing I could think of:

"Umm, actually he passed away."

This, I have learned, elicits many people's interests, usually with respect, although asking a thirteen-year-old

"How?"

is something I'd stay away from, unless it is important, or if you know that they are comfortable talking about it. At the time, I was completely uncomfortable talking about it—for fuck sakes, I couldn't even understand it until years later. And despite my discomfort, I also learned that it is sometimes better to lie about certain causes of death for reasons that hopefully will become nonexistent . . . because when I was thirteen, if I replied,

"Suicide."

even some of the most socially attentive adults would be lost for words. Thus, just a few interactions taught me to instead reply,

"It was an accident."

And with that line, I would swiftly change the topic to avoid awkward condolences and my own blushing face.

I assume that some people ask about the cause of death in an attempt to sympathize or relate to the situation (since they too lost someone to cancer, a heart attack, and so on . . .). But I would caution you to ask only if you are prepared to carry the conversation on, without making things uncomfortable, after hearing about something you wouldn't expect. Thankfully, I now believe that I have mastered the art of talking about death, suicide, grief, and everything in between (writing about it definitely helped), but that isn't the case for everyone. So, ensuring that you are aware of people's comfort, and whether they seem like they want to avoid those conversations, is essential (for instance, instead of asking, "How?" maybe try, "Are you comfortable telling me how they died?" so that people do not feel extra pressure to speak about something that they don't want to, and they can feel comforted by the more empathetic way of asking). It might even be helpful to ask yourself why you are inclined to hear about the cause of death. That answer could give you better direction on whether you should ask or not. And since not all people will respond to these questions the way you or I do, I think it is just a good idea to consistently try our best to mitigate the potential harm that we could cause someone by ensuring comfort (and escape hatches) in these conversations.

On another note, if you feel reluctant to talk to others about death and grief, YOU ARE NOT ALONE. These are challenging subjects whose conversations are flawed by the ways that society lacks understanding and empathy. I still lie, often, about what happened to my dad even though I am comfortable talking about it. Because some people don't need to know, and sometimes, you don't need to share, and sometimes, I think that the lie is true because *he had an accident in his head*.

YOU ARE RESILIENT

You opened your eyes to a new day
and familiar routine proceeded
But the air didn't satisfy your breath
and your eyes screamed uncertainty
So when you got home
and the house had collapsed
You learned how to be resilient

Your restless night
showered into a field of agony
Because you knew something was wrong
long before the words arrived at your door
Then time stopped and you cried for hours
as your mind kept screaming
You need to be resilient

You were over the mountains with a moment's notice
presents filled with your hands and your heart
Though every muscle cramped labouring your pain
you mended the wounds they couldn't
And before the home could start crashing into waves
your anchors laid on the ocean floor
Grounding them in your resilience

You started to drive the straight road ahead
to join the weeping home
Lingering trauma fogging your mind
a pain you'd never wished for your child
And you strive to be strong
though your heart breaks twice
Showing your forms of resilience

So were you

You battled demons in silence
while giving us beautiful lives
But each of our timelines will differ
and resilience is not absent in loss
Though clouds of anguish make it hard to see
your resiliency shined in a different way
Because through it all
we have no doubt
You were resilient

You Are Resilient. Ooof. This statement elicits the full colour wheel of emotions. For many reasons I love this statement, and for the same and other reasons, I hate it. And as I have mentioned, until just one round of edits before publishing this book, that was what it was called. But after some reflection, and heated internal debates, I realized that this book wasn't going to be an autopsy of resiliency, and it wasn't trying to be a self-help, confidence-boosting remedy for life. So, I instead opted for the rawer and more genuine This Grief Thing F**KING Sucks. But the previous title was derived from this poem because it was one of my first poems and it was one that I both loved and hated, as the ideas surrounding resiliency are things that I both love and hate. I love that resiliency is subjective; there is no minimum threshold to be resilient. In fact, everyone is resilient. And throughout life with grief, I've benefitted from being reminded that I am resilient because it gives me validation in the difficult situations that I've battled to get to where I presently am. But on the same note, the number of times that I was told I was strong or resilient when I was in an extremely dark place was deafening. It made me want to scream "It's just an act!" and that I wanted help, but I wasn't comfortable asking for it because I'd been conditioned by compliments of resilience to think that it was the only way I should behave. This is one of the major flaws with how our society treats grief. When someone dies, we expect resilience. We expect them to be strong, and to get through it. In fact, society only gives us that option because when you aren't resilient, you are judged, outcasted, "sensitive," without work, without resources, and unable to carry on with life as many of us know it. Another issue that I have with being considered resilient is the consequential tokenization of my resiliency being used to pressure others into "resilience." I believe that it is never okay to expect someone to think and act similarly to another person no matter how analogous their situations may be. We are an incredibly complex species whose emotions and abilities are dictated by a nearly unpredictable combination of genes and experiences. Not only has my resiliency been depicted by my unique genes and experiences, but I have also been very fortunate to have many resources and tools for grief that so many people may never have—it would be a complete disgrace to ignore this nuance and expect other people to respond to loss in the way that I, or anyone else, has. But I have seen it done, and I was guilty of doing it until I realized how much harm praising resiliency caused others, as well myself. So, although resiliency can be a welcome compliment to some, I also think it is important to be aware of the ways in which it can be harmful and cause pain to others.

~

Trying to look beyond your perspective on a hardship can be very painful—not losing sight of your own situation but allowing yourself to empathize with others. It hurts. Sometimes it hurts more than living in your own sorrows, to venture out into that of others . . . maybe that's why many are reluctant to empathize. I say this because I have struggled to metaphorically step into the shoes of others, often finding myself overwhelmed by what it could have been like to be them. And although I will never truly understand how others feel, I realized that to be better to those around me and to accept my own experiences I needed to try. This poem was one of those attempts. In each stanza, I attempted to provide a different perspective of the day that Dad died. And in doing so, I found myself having a greater appreciation for the intentions of others, and I was able to let go of some of the frustrations that I had toward them. It also allowed me to remember the day better—what had happened and why I had certain feelings about the events. Though I still find it difficult to move around the lenses that I see life through, writing poems like this, and talking with people about how they feel, has taught me how to empathize in a much more meaningful way and give others the benefit of the doubt in all situations. But holy fuck, it's difficult when so many of the systems that we operate in are inherently judgmental and assume that set solutions will work for everyone. At least when it comes to our battles with grief, let's let go of our judgment and support each other in finding the solutions that work for each of us (though I see no reason not to apply this in all areas of life too . . .).

WELCOME

Welcome to the community,
of grievers.

Where the walls are littered with images
of those we miss,
and the memories that remain.
Where everyone has unfortunately,
had to meet me.
Inside the air is warm
but the drafts are cold,
the highs will shine
while the lows steal your breath.
And from piece to piece
you'll have to trek,
until you find what you need.

And although you may feel alone
you roam the gallery together,
this endlessly growing community
becoming everyone's reality.
Find those that you resonate with,
those you can walk with silently,
or take a moment to enjoy
the thoughts of your own company.
Looking at the murals around the room
for hints to try to understand me,
I'll try to give you what you need,
but grieving is never easy.

Though these rooms, walls, and the art
symbolize a cluster of emotions,
I brought you here to try and make sure
you find some grief companions.
Cause when I knock you down,
step on your glasses,
and make you lose your way,
this community will lend its hand to make sure
that you're going to be okay.

So, welcome to the community,
of grievers.

Just as this poem says, I say to you: welcome. Welcome to these conversations, these poems, and stories. Welcome to the community of grievers, open to anyone, and where we are all working to understand our grief. Grief itself welcomes grievers to the community, but you may also find it on a journey to learn about grief or a journey to prepare yourself for grief. And maybe more people should learn, because the world is cold to grievers, yet grief is in every corner of this world. Not always the people, but our systems and our societies have been built to ignore grief. So, grief is a topic kept quiet, full of shadows and silence. It's not usually a topic that you will find yourself advocating for or against, or chatting about at a coffee shop, but maybe now it will be. Because now that we are learning about it, we can become more comfortable with it. And I hope that by learning we won't hesitate to talk to our friends, family members, and colleagues about grief, asking about their experiences or sharing our own. Hopefully we will learn to understand how to help someone who is grieving, help ourselves grieve, and make life an easier place to grieve. So, again, welcome to the community, and thank you for coming!

~

Something I discovered when I lost Dad was how quickly I grasped onto or noticed those around me who "got it." The other grievers. These are the people who see that you just joined the club, who are waiting for you at the door. They show up every day, they are friendly, and they want to hear how you are doing. Some resent being in the community. Some are there because they have to be. Others are trying to join because a friend referred them, or they are seeing someone in the community. When I realized this invisible grief community existed, I found it so interesting. I'd now found myself in this community, brought here by grief, and

I was now noticing and gravitating toward others who were also in the club. I noticed that some people who reached out, just by the way that they did, were familiar with grief. Or I would find myself drawn toward people who are in the community, even before I even found out that they were a part of it. Appreciatively, grief has connected me to wonderful people and allowed me to build relationships that help me grieve.

Thinking about grief as a community has also helped me to understand more about grief. For one, by realizing the vast number of ways that people react to loss, learning other theories about grief, and hearing about other experiences has made me more comfortable with my own. And oh my gosh, it's so validating to hear that other people struggle with the same things I do. Like how they hate Christmas because it's hard to escape feeling lonely or stop yourself from longing for the Christmas from five years ago. Or how they struggle to define boundaries with those who ignore our grief, yet who themselves are grieving. Knowing that I am not alone with these troubles, and learning about how others manage theirs, has really helped me to become a more confident and healthier griever. So, thankfully, this community has made me a better griever for myself and, I believe, a better friend to grievers.

~

After Dad died, there were a few people who really understood, who came and embraced new roles in our lives. They helped us, and gave us space, they left dinners on the porch and expected nothing in return. These were the people that made grieving easier, that allowed us to take more time for ourselves, to plan and digest. Not to worry about the little details, like sending a thank you or a message, just helping with the intention to help us, not to help themselves.

These were our angels, and they continue to be our angels. They support us from afar, offer assistance when they can, send a package or a note expecting nothing but to reduce some of our hurt. And, likely, this is one way that the grieving community really helps each other: They know how they would want to help themselves.

Even years after losing Dad, I found myself drawn toward people that I had no idea were a part of this community. Maybe it's because these people seemed to view otherwise ordinary events similarly, understanding their value in a different way. Or maybe the people I was drawn to in this invisible community have similar zests for life, knowing firsthand that it could be gone in an instant.

WHAT WILL IT

It doesn't get easier
it just becomes normal.
Pieces that have shattered,
still fit together.
Memories remain,
but what can we actually see
of memories?
Deep inside I lie,
it will become easier.

It will become easier
as you become stronger.
Each time you fall,
you can get back up.
Choose to get up,
because we are built to survive
a hard life.
Deep inside I lie,
it doesn't get easier.

The poem "What Will It" represents the unsung background music to my mom's demeanour as she continued moving forward with dad's death. Given numerous changes, new responsibilities, and the pressure to adequately guide her two young daughters, Mom had to learn how to grieve amid nothing less than chaos. Her journey navigating grief was resilient and nurturing despite her deep sorrow and fear. In writing this poem and these details, I hope to encompass the version of grief and the perspectives on grief that I believe my mom embraced in order to keep herself and us pointed toward happy and healthy lives.

When Dad passed away, Mom became our sole caregiver, support, parent, and love. This is a ridiculous amount to put onto anyone's plate. But it gave me a front row seat to witness the immense strength and empathy exhibited by widowed and single parents. Having to support themselves, while also being the primary support for their families, is a battle these warriors fight around the clock. And Mom did it with grace, by learning to understand and move forward with the abounding amounts of grief that came with losing the love of her life while caring for her two young daughters. Incredibly, she handled every hurdle that came her way, teaching us that we don't always have to jump over it, but that we can walk around it—or knock it down—because no matter how we addressed the race, just continuing was the victory. I couldn't have been given a better role model for how to address grief and death. Mom modelled strength, though she also showed us that it was okay to cry. She gave us confidence, but she also gave us room to be insecure. She taught us to love the world, even though we had thousands of reasons to hate it. She assured us that however we needed to grieve was the right way, and she would be there for whatever we needed to get through another day. She taught me to talk about all of it, by talking to me about all of it—by being vulnerable herself. But most admirably, Mom continued to remind us of the wonderful father we once had, that we were so lucky to have for as long as we did, and who will continue to shape some of the best parts of our lives. It is because of all of these things that I can wake up and live a life I enjoy.

~

Undoubtedly, I may have given Mom a much harder time then I should have, not even understanding what a breakup felt like, never mind losing your husband in such a traumatic way. When she started to date, I reasonably felt a bit uncomfortable, but I didn't try to empathize with her. I thought it wasn't fair to Sam or me, I thought that it would prompt negative opinions about her relationship with Dad. But I was so wrong, so disillusioned by traditional concepts of marriage and grief to think that it was about Dad when all along it was about Mom. She had no one; she went from sharing everything to sharing nothing and taking everything, and then some, onto her plate. She had to give so much support to Sam and me; I have no doubt she didn't have enough for herself at the end of the day. Had I known what it felt like to need support like that, to lose love, comfort, and stability, I would have never said the stupid things I did. I mean, maybe that's a big part of what immaturity is—the inability to empathize with another perspective. And on top of the guilt that I'd made her feel, Sam and I definitely did not make single parenting easy for her (I have no doubt that the "teenage phase" was a bulldozer on her sanity), but thankfully we all came out of it better (I think). Honestly, I have no idea how Mom did it all. She had to take over everything Dad did for us—organize school and co-curricular activities, take care of the house, parent two daughters, support us financially—all while dealing with a form of grief that I could never comprehend. Mom, like all widows and single parents, was a fucking rockstar.

~

On a side note, I want to point out that you can approach and understand this poem in many different ways, which I think mirrors the different forms that grief can embody throughout life. Mom wanted us to grieve in any way that we wanted to; she understood the importance of vulnerability, of questioning, of sitting with the uniqueness of your own grief. So, when you read it top-to-bottom-left-to-right-as-two-stanzas, it still leaves enough vagueness for you to fill in the holes as to how you would grieve. But it can also be read top-to-bottom-left-to-right-as-one-stanza, telling us more directly that there are different mindsets to each situation. And reading it the opposite ways could resonate with those who continue to struggle to make sense of their grief, and to those, like myself, who don't believe things "get easier."

A WIDOW, A WARRIOR

How do you tell your babies
their dad is gone
How do you tell yourself
you will be okay
How do you move forward
when time has stopped
How do you explain something
they may never understand
How do you wake up and smile
when everything has changed
How do you sleep alone
for the very first time
knowing that this is it

I guess it goes without saying, but Mom had to be strong as hell. She had to do unimaginable things, at the expense of her own happiness, to ensure Sam and I were able to take on life. I can't imagine how I would prepare myself to tell my children that their father had died. Or how I would begin to explain to them the concept of suicide, especially having never been so close to the topic and never having to engage with what it meant. Amid your own shock, heartbreak, and fear, you now had to induce the same pain in your babies? Like, how do we act so strongly while we are so weak? How does numbing the pain allow us to keep going? I mean, it's inevitable, the pain and hurt—maybe it's just a bittersweet part of the fight to survive—but damn, it really fucking sucks.

Mom fought hard after Dad died. She fought for all of us, and she had to, because the world is cold to grievers. Though she struggled with her heartbreak and guilty thoughts—that as a nurse she should have realized what was going on—though she struggled to sleep, to eat, to give love and to receive love, she still made sure Sam and I had everything we needed. I don't know where her strength came from. And although she had some amazing friends, support, and resources, it wasn't all as good as it could have been. Months and years later, as if her grief had gone away, support began to dwindle. And I think that this is where the essence of her strength was revealed. She lacked the support she wanted, and she was hurt by those close to her, yet she kept her hopes high. Maybe they were unable to empathize with her situation or unable to realize what was going on. It seemed like people didn't see her perspective, and they didn't give her the credit that she deserved. As though she could somehow "get over" the loss of her partner, her best friend, and the father of her children. She'd had a partner for nearly two decades, yet being alone is something that she could easily learn, value, and accept. And she'd had a partner because she valued relationships, because she valued interdependency and support. So how can we expect all of these things to easily change? In just a matter of months or in just a matter of years? It usually takes people decades to realize and then change parts of themselves, but because we shouldn't dwell on death, Mom was expected to change the core aspects of who she was and how she operated in just a couple years? This is where society is cold to grievers; we are cold to each other when we lack the ability to empathize. Maybe it's evidence of the rotten narcissism epidemic or maybe we just generally fail to try to empathize. It's as though people expect grievers to change gracefully, to grieve gracefully, or to just fall from grace.

It still baffles me that friends and family expected Mom to behave in certain ways, to do or not do certain things. They failed to empathize with her extremely traumatizing and heartbreaking situation. One memory that will stay with me forever comes from a night when Mom opened up to me about this. For years after Dad died, Mom and I would sleep together; she had a TV in her room, so we would watch shows and movies until we fell asleep. I was having nightmares and she was having difficulties sleeping, so it was comforting for both of us. One night, I came to sleep in her room and noticed that she had been crying hard (you know the eyes). She didn't cry like this often, especially in front of myself or Sam—rather, she usually saved her fat tears and loud cries for when we were away. Worried, I asked her what was happening, and she fought back more tears. She never wanted to burden us with her heartache, but I insisted, and I think she knew she needed the support. She said she was having a "pity party" because she hadn't been able to find friends to go to the movies with her. She and Dad used to go to the movies together pretty frequently. I have no doubt that she was missing those dates and that part of her lifestyle. Mom also said that she was upset because her friends who were "coupled up" had slowly decreased the number of times they would invite her to hang out with them. Whether it was something she did, or her "vibe," it's hard to escape the thought that it could be because she was coming alone. She was so sad, and she was so lonely, but maybe her strong front gave her friends the impression that she was okay. But let me tell you, she was so fucking sad. This was the first time in months that I saw Mom's heartbreak. And my God, does it kill you to realize your mom is hurting. Seeing her heart continue to break every time she wanted to do something that they would have done together, every time she felt alone or scared . . . you could hear the sadness being masked in her voice. We would be driving somewhere, driving for a couple of hours, and when the conversations ended, and the music got boring, you'd see tears begin to roll down her cheeks. The thoughts are inescapable years later, maybe forever—and that is what we fail to recognize, what we fail to verbalize. But I hope that now, by telling these stories, I can help illuminate to friends and families of grievers that things don't just get better; they get easier as you become stronger, but we can't always expect ourselves to be strong.

~

Watching Mom's response to losing Dad demonstrated how exceedingly complicated life-altering grief is; it changes your lifestyle, your decisions, your goals, and you, in a deeply personal way. Mom exemplified courage, benevolence, and humour, finding her unique ways to continue on. She would have a few glasses of wine, laugh as loud as she wanted, go gliding, and poke fun at those around her. She found her ways to keep living. Now, this does not sound like the description of a "widow," does it? Rather, Mom shattered the stereotyped media portrayal of widows as pessimistic, bitter, and malicious with her optimism, affection, and her smile. And maybe this is just what we needed, what we all need—a reminder that "widow" is not synonymous with sadness, but strength.

OUR MENTAL HEALTH

i'm struggling a bit mentally
but aren't we all
for what makes up normal
nobody can tell
but we continue to learn
and continue to try
by helping each other
to figure out why
it's a delicate balance
keeping us alive
allowing us to be playful
and able to thrive
but sometimes meds don't help
and these feelings arise
let's talk to each other
time to empathize
so we can start to know
different paths and points
so we can start to grow

so we can help ourselves
and then we can show
our successes and our strengths
and say good-bye to our woes
once we work on ourselves
and help each other
we'll break out of our shells
and stand together
so, talk to your friends
and spill the drama
tell them you're angry
or tell them your trauma
talk about therapy
and talk about your worry
because once we can talk freely
it will lessen our fury
so, let's normalize mourning
let's eliminate othering
time to build a community
that validates suffering

A conversation that we cannot neglect when we talk about grief is that of mental health. Honestly, mental health is not something that I am completely comfortable writing about. Given I am not a trained professional, or versed in academia on the topic, there is only so much I can say with confidence. For one, I can't teach you about the intricacies of how the brain functions, but I can try to explain how mental health has affected and been affected by my grief. Additionally, since Dad died by suicide, conversations about mental health, and working to understand suicidal acts, have been a large part of my life. I hope that by sharing glimpses into some of these discussions, I can contribute to fostering environments that help people optimize their mental health, especially when faced with grief.

On one hand, grief—and the events that cause grief—seems to be a catalyst for worsening mental health. I find that the presence of grief challenges the stability of my mental health. The influx of sadness makes the fight for happiness harder, and grief's looming presence makes it hard to forget the emotions that came with it. To expect our mental health to be unwavering when its new friend grief is consistently serving chaotic sad energy is asking far too much. It's no surprise that we may find ourselves affected by depression, anxiety, or other conditions when grief consumes large parts of our lives.

Not only does the sadness, heartbreak, and fear brought about by grief affect mental health, but I have also found that the way I learned to cope with grief shaped parts of my mental health. For instance, one of my responses to loss was anxiety-driven, out of the general feeling of instability in my life. To cope with this anxiety, I would assert control and display a facade of confidence. I wanted to be in control of anything that I could, and I was comfortable doing that because I was certain of myself and my abilities. My need to be in control and this fake confidence soon became my first lines of defence against grief or any other challenges to my mental health. But unfortunately, I have found that grief's strong interference in my mental health limited my ability to be truly healthy. For instance, my need to be in control didn't lessen or prevent my anxiety, it just shifted the anxiety elsewhere. My need for control also caused me to lack trust, influencing (usually negatively) how I navigated relationships. Additionally, employing confidence in situations where I was feeling hurt, or experiencing grief, lead to unnecessary overconfidence, since no amount of confidence could really satisfy or battle these feelings. And it is a dangerous game using confidence, especially fake confidence, as a tool in emotional battles. For instance, it would cause me to gaslight myself, saying that I am being too sensitive, that I shouldn't feel so hurt, and that I am too strong to let grief affect me. All that this did was prolong the hurt that grief caused me, never finding a way to prevent the hurt in the first place. And this confidence—leading the way to narcissism—would hurt others as well, manipulating them as I did myself, positing truth in nuanced conversations, and changing narratives so that I couldn't really see how things were affecting me or others. It wasn't until I began to address my grief that the need for control, and this outward display of confidence, began diminishing. Though I am still working on it, I found that in order to manage the anxiety that grief caused me, I needed to address the root—the feeling of instability. Just by accepting that my anxiety was driven by feelings of instability, I was able to make changes to my life, the way I lived, and who I surrounded myself with to mitigate how often I felt unstable. Then, when instability does surface, I have more genuine confidence in my ability to regain stability: not the kind of confidence that is masking insecurity, but the kind that accepts that though it won't be perfect, we will find a way to make things better.

~

Another way that grief relates to mental health is through their mutual friend trauma. Undoubtedly, trauma causes a whirlwind of confusion and change to one's mental health, but what I find interesting is how closely connected trauma and grief are. Not only does grief often accompany trauma, but grief itself can be quite traumatic. It's almost as though trauma and grief run with each other as they both emerge after a loss.

When Dad died, hearing that he had died, seeing everyone's reactions, and trying to navigate my response was reasonably traumatic. To this day, I get anxious thinking about the day and how I went about talking to friends and family afterward. Because of the trauma that's associated with most of our grief, I understand why we may not talk about death and grief frequently, why these conversations are notoriously awkward and difficult to navigate. We should never want to re-traumatize others or ourselves, but when grief and trauma as so closely connected, how can we talk about one without the other? For me, I wasn't comfortable talking about it until recently, until I felt in control of both my grief and my trauma. So even though I am encouraging these conversations, I want to be mindful that not everyone is going to be ready yet, and not everyone is going to want to—and that is so okay.

~

After Dad died, we began questioning whether he may have been influenced by a type of mood disorder; this would help to explain his moods, mania, and possibly a part of his choice. Although, it doesn't really matter what his diagnosis would have been (if he'd had any). What matters is that he didn't access help, and conversations about mental health and suicide were not in abundance. And frankly, it's common for men, especially men my dad's age, to be undiagnosed or unaware of a mental health status and its role in overall health and happiness. Hopefully this is changing for younger men, but I also hope that conversations and shared education will help men in my dad's generation ask for help and start thinking about their own mental health.

Before Dad passed, Mom had noticed that he wasn't as happy as he used to be; he was becoming very quick-tempered and distant, she thought that it must have had to do with her, his work, or their love. They went to couples counselling and they began working through their troubles, but it soon became clear that the issues were not with their marriage—rather, Dad was struggling with something far worse. But he never talked about it, he didn't open up about it, and we never imagined that thoughts of suicide were on the horizon. Dad fit the stereotype of a jock; he oozed athleticism and cool despite his few dorky qualities. As a man of few words, but many actions, his tough and cool nature might have been his fatal flaw. Mom said she had only ever seen him cry twice in his life, and I don't remember him ever talking about his emotions. I now realize those are flags—flags that, even if someone is mentally well, demonstrate that you'll never know if they aren't. Mom was a nurse, and she and Dad were going to a marriage counsellor, yet his struggles with mental health went unnoticed. But maybe that is just how mental health works—unless you can talk about it, no one will really know. So, as I've expressed in this poem, I urge you to talk about it if you are comfortable; talk about it with your friends and your family. Take the first step and be vulnerable so others feel like they can be too.

~

Dad's choice may have been different if he hadn't been living during a time where stigma filled conversations about mental health and where social norms told men to be emotionless. Society idealized and fetishized the tough guys, the jocks, the emotionally unavailable; but then, we have men struggling in silence and being picked on for displaying their emotions. Societies, historically and presently, have demonstrated disfavour toward people with mental health disorders or towards those who live with suicidal thoughts or behaviour. It was, and often still is, common for people to view those deemed mentally unwell or who live with suicidal thoughts or behaviours as being inhuman and broken: thoughts that are far from the truth and nothing but harmful, contributing to further neglect, insufficient resources, and a lack of support for everyone to live healthily. So, how do we move away from this? How do we help each other and mitigate the harm we cause each other? We could default our blame on society, on the stigma around mental health, especially male mental health, but blame alone won't change these situations for others. Working toward changing the stigmas, by talking about mental health, about death, about suicide, and grief—that's a starting point. Because the truth is, it's on us to prioritize these conversations, to decide enough is enough. To know that it's not okay to poke fun at men who are more sensitive than the stereotype. Or that we should be conscious of how we talk about suicide every day. It's on us to prioritize these conversations about our own moods and emotions so that when the time comes, others feel comfortable to do so as well. I think the time has long come to do our best every day to avoid contributing to the problem that took my dad and many, many people since. And I want to acknowledge that in last ten years, since Dad's death, some incredible work has significantly contributed to destigmatizing mental health and suicide in the communities I engage with. But there is no end to the amount of work that we can do to ensure the health and happiness of those around us.

Beyond just talking about mental health and suicide, I believe that to work toward creating safer spaces for others, we need to work on our own trauma, so we don't continue to traumatize. We need to learn how to navigate and create comfortable conversations, without taking up too much space, all while remaining meaningfully engaged. When we have safe spaces in which to speak and exist, we can be informed and find better ways to help those around us. In the same vein, I have no doubt that every single person can benefit from customized therapy or counselling because there is no such thing as a perfect parent or a perfect life. We are all affected by trauma or harm, and it influences us in countless ways. If the reasons behind what we do are a product of our genes and experiences, then by analyzing, reflecting, and removing or introducing new things we can alter gene expressions, responses to triggers, and find ways to protect and strengthen ourselves. There is always opportunity to be better people: better for our friends, our families, our communities, and for ourselves; but we can't better ourselves without change. So, maybe it all begins with us, working on changing ourselves.

~

Another concept that I was hoping this poem would capture is how our trauma and our mental health status can be hindering our help and causing immense harm to one another. What I mean by this is that the help we intend for each other may not be materializing because of the ways that our trauma interferes. We may be unintentionally harming each other because of what we have going on mentally. Though we may have great intentions, it seems like until you've helped yourself, or until you are at least aware of your traumas and flaws, you will not be able to offer the entirety of yourself to help those around you. I am not saying that this is necessary, but to an extent it means that by helping ourselves we are also likely to help those around us by increasing the amount of help we provide and decreasing the harm we inflict on one another. I think realizing this is crucial, when it comes to mental health, and it is crucial when it comes to grief. The people who are still learning how to be healthy as they grieve and who are emotionally suffering, are not always going to be able to help without hurting. And I know this firsthand because I was not the person I wanted to be for my sister or my mother after Dad died. I didn't know any better at the time, though I wish I had. I couldn't see the ways that my grief and trauma were blurring my intentions so that I was unable to help them or treat them the way I wanted. It took years of hard conversations and therapy for me to begin recognizing my flaws and see some of the ways I was causing harm. At some point, I realized that I did nothing but hurt my sister when I would criticize her choices. And I hurt my mom when I would tell her she was acting inappropriately. Even if my intentions were to help them, it did nothing but hurt them. So, that's when I realized I needed to change, to be more thoughtful. And it hasn't been easy. I still find myself reverting to anger, to vanity, and to pride when I'm overwhelmed, but by continuing to be aware and practise healthy habits, I believe that I have diminished the amount of hurt I've caused. Similarly, there have been many people in my life whose intentions were very pure, but their actions were clouded by their own grief and trauma, causing harm in situations that needn't have been harmful. To this day, some people choose not to work on it, and that's okay—that's out of our control. But also minimizing the opportunities for these people to hurt us is important for our own growth, for our own grief, and for our own happiness.

WHERE DID YOU GO

Look left and look right
Nowhere in sight
Look up and look down
Nowhere in town
Look high and look low
Nowhere to go
Just leaving us to be;
Sad?

Come here or go there
Where is the air?
It's near and it's dear
Why is there fear?
Too late it's fate
How long is the wait?
When you've left us to be;
Mad?

Good grief could be my lousy motif
That actualizes a happiness thief
Bringing forward another belief
Making the encounter utterly brief
Never offering any relief
For the grief

Good grief

"Where Did You Go" highlights the numerous feelings and abundant questions that can arise in response to loss. Especially at 13, these feelings and questions felt endless. It was like I was standing at the base of a tornado watching and feeling all the parts of my life twirl around me as I tried to make sense of what was happening. Dad in one way was gone, but in another still with me. He would drift into my vision throughout the day, randomly, and be gone again in a second. My thoughts, my emotions, and my reactions were tangled amidst the debris circling me, but just out of my reach. I couldn't predict when I would be reminded of Dad, when I would feel the heartbreak, or when I would become anxious about who else would die around me. I did the only thing I could to continue moving forward: I tried my best to ignore it. But by ignoring it, I never got used to the feelings; I never allowed myself to embrace them, so when a wave would come stronger than my walls could withstand, I would break. It was all or nothing when it came to grief in my teens.

~

After reflecting on how grief has affected me throughout different periods of my life, I noticed a unique connection between my grief and my mental health; I found that I had begun to grieve the loss of mental health. The loss of mental health? I guess I mean the loss of a healthier mind or the loss of the ability to control and understand an unhealthy mind. Where the healthy mind, the healthy thoughts, and the healthy habits were suddenly missing—reality is slipping, and you feel as though your health, your control, these parts of you, have been stolen by grief. I didn't know when or how it happened, but when I realized that my mind wasn't operating in a healthy way, greater pain came with each visit from grief. And it makes sense that grief had slowly and secretly eroded my lines of defence, as I didn't work on strengthening my mental health. I thought I was invincible, utterly resilient, but that couldn't have been farther from the truth. In high school it was hard to make time for grief and mental health while wanting to play sports, go out, meet people, and do well in classes. Reasonably, by ignoring grief, and allowing it to chip away at my mental health, I found as time went on that things were not getting better. In fact, I was becoming far more impatient, entitled, and ignorant. Grief hurt more as time went on, and I grieved how I used to be mentally stronger and in better control of myself. Though grief is likely one contributing factor to these feelings and my actions, I noticed that when I began accepting grief's role in my life, everything else began to smooth out as well. But I'll go into more detail later about how I began to manage grief and its relationship with my mental health.

PILLOW

As feathers filled my ears,
it was like I was there, or like you were here.

Wind gusts ruffled our clothes,
but hushed the moment you said hello.

Reminded of how it felt to see your face,
summoned shivers I refused to embrace.

And my mind battled the flutters filling my core,
while I hoped I could stay just a little while more.

But gone again in a second
leaving me to dwell on the thoughts.
To crave the sensations
of the life that you'd brought us.

That morning I woke tearful
and I still wake in a pillow of tears.
Because it's a foul trick
letting me sniff the moment I've wanted for years.

Dreams can be some of the best and worst experiences for people who are grieving. Dreams allow us to relive moments, to recall memories in different ways, and to form new ones. But when dreams are one of our only means to form new memories of someone, they can become a bittersweet experience. Since Dad died, I have had many dreams of our family together; riding bikes or getting ice cream. But these dreams feel so different from most others; they feel euphoric. They are so good I could cry, while also tearing at the stitches that hold my heart together. There are times I've woken up and bawled until my eyes swell shut. To see him, to hear him, to be with him—it's like the drug I've been deprived of. A single moment just leaves me wanting more. Then all the emotions that I've had after losing Dad spiral through my mind at once, unable to organize themselves. Each dream displaces my mind, causing a wave of grief. And somehow, in these dreams, I know he's dead—maybe it is the shock of seeing him—yet we continue on like no time has passed. To this day, when I have dreams and Dad is there, I can't help but love them to the point that I cry; and then continue crying because of how much I hate them.

I sometimes wonder if I had the choice, whether I would choose not to have these dreams. Do they hurt me more than they help?

IT'S NOT ABOUT WHAT YOU SAY

A hug that lasts a lifetime,
lingers, unexplainable.
Maybe it's not about what you say,
but how you make them feel.

The moment filled with sensitive tides,
timelessly, recycling.
Memory whispers pain,
humbly, suffocating.

Feelings left untouched by words,
voices, inarticulate.
An essence unable to be captured,
emotionally, infinite.

The care, the love, the hurt, and the grief,
encompassed in that moment,
gave me something beyond comfort,
and feelings of condolence.

Though things were blurry,
and my mind was weak,
that simple hug was promising.

The racing stopped,
emotions fled,
sadness finally materializing.

I cried in your arms,
empty, vulnerable,
and your strength began to recharge me.

You let me breathe,
and gave me time,
providing all forms of stability.

But so many years later,
I still feel the strength,
that you gave me in that hug.

I remember the feelings,
and stop to breathe,
knowing that I am loved.

How do I thank you for that moment,
for all the things it's given me?
Even if it was just that moment
it's become a part of me, eternally.

In the weeks following Dad's death, I was in a state of shock. Unable to understand my thoughts, trying my best to make sense of the situation . . . everything was thoroughly numb. It struck me that I could feel emotionless, yet full of emotions, as though they were all fighting to take control, leaving me utterly confused. Days and nights blurred, and to this day, memories of the months that followed are nearly unavailable . . . except this one moment—a breakthrough, a realization, and a breakdown. Nights after hearing about Dad, I was up and unable to sleep because of a war going on inside my head.

> "Am I the reason that this happened?"
> "Was it something I said? Was it something I did?"
> "Did Mom know? Did anyone know?"
> "Were we not enough?"
> "Will I ever do something like that?"

The world inside my head began to spiral, warping my thoughts and leaving me in a trance. Most likely these thoughts put me on the verge of a panic attack, wanting to make sense of the situation but knowing I may never be able to. Unfortunately, this is a situation that many grievers may understand, when the room starts to feel small, mind flooding with memories both good and bad, and you're holding back tears that you know you won't be able to control once you let go. Though it was late, and I didn't want to wake anyone, I had to leave my room, take a walk, catch my breath, and get a drink. I walked upstairs, clenching my teeth and trying to find anything that would distract me. But then I heard footsteps coming down the hall and before turning to see who it was, I tried to convince myself that I was alright, that I was just grabbing some water—I really didn't want to cause anyone extra distress that night. But it was my aunt. The one who had flown in, who kept groceries in the fridge, who was doing our laundry, and who to this day is an angel in our lives. Before saying anything that I can remember, we walked toward each other, and I fell into her arms. The hug felt timeless as the chaos inside began to settle like dust, until sadness stood there, alone. I began to cry, fat tears rolling off my face, because I finally felt sad—not confused, not worried, not anxious, or scared—just sad. As far as I remember, she said nothing and held me tight; it was as if she knew that this was what I needed. Maybe it was because she was sad too; she had just lost her brother, and despite the incredible strength she showed every day making sure everyone else was alright, the air of sadness in our house felt inescapable. I think it was what we both needed, that hug. During the silence of the night, through the break of emotions, and with the last bit of strength I could forge, it gave me the energy I needed to breathe.

Throughout life, we encounter things that are hard to explain, hard to describe in words, and for me, this hug was one of those things. It was an action that has sat with me, that I can continue to feel, and that still helps me to breathe. Maybe it's the optimism that there are good people, that things will be okay, or that I am loved. This hug captures the philosophy that my mom encouraged: *It's not about what you say, but it's about how you make them feel*. To this day, I don't know what words were, or were not, exchanged during this hug, but I remember clear as present how it made me feel.

And this philosophy has felt quite accurate for most of the condolatory encounters I have had—I remember the feelings, both positive and negative, but not always the words or actions that aroused those feelings. It's funny how quickly we will associate people with the way they have made us feel, for reasons that we may forget, but some part of us doesn't. Knowing this, the importance of feelings, in making someone feel better, has helped me in my efforts to be a better friend to those who are grieving. I know I don't need to find the perfect words, or the perfect gift—as long as my intentions are to genuinely help and to make the person feel better in a meaningful way. I always appreciated the people who were mindful of my experience, who centered me in their attempts to help, and who ensured maximal comfort so that I could grieve. Now I try to do that for others, but I recognize this may not be the route to helping all grievers. So when I am unsure (as I often am) I try checking in with them, and I try to create a safe space where they can say how they would like to be helped. For instance, some people are nonconfrontational; they won't tell you if they don't want you doing something or if they don't feel comfortable. As friends of grievers, we need to be aware of that. We need make sure that they know it's okay to set the boundaries they want, and that we will respect those boundaries. Because if I am honestly trying to make someone feel better, I must first respect their wants and needs. But in order to do so, I need to put that person before myself and do what I can to make them comfortable. I think that it is important to provide agency to people healing, so that they can heal in a way that doesn't re-traumatize them and helps them move forward in their journey. Mom tried to do this for Sam and me, despite our younger ages she knew that we needed to have control over how we grieved. She would reassure us that it is okay to say anything we wanted, that we weren't going to hurt her feelings, and that she was there to help in any way or fashion. One thing I've learned to say that often helps and brings a room full of smiles is that I would be honoured to be their figurative punching bad. If they just need someone to scream at or to say all the things that they are supressing to, I would be so happy to be that for them. And of course, if they just want space, then it is all theirs and

I'll happy write the note for the door that says, "Currently Unavailable". Ultimately, we will never know exactly what to do, or how to help, so making sure that they know you are 100% there for them, that you are open to any form of helping—without judgment—and that you are present with the intention of being the friend they need are the only ways we can fully help each other. Also, in my personal experience, actions speak louder than words. If you want to help someone who has just experienced a loss, bringing them meals, offering to pick up groceries, or finding ways to minimize public exposure can be some beautiful ways to mitigate their hurt.

WHERE WE ARE NOW

Maybe it's in my blood
The ability to grieve
A requirement of race
Why I have these beliefs
This loss of identity
And our communal hurt
Taught us resiliency
And to head down, work
It's a system of errors
Producing more flaws
Preying on barriers
Masking the cause
To survive, look high
Reach for the shelves
Hurting each other
Or hurting ourselves
Maybe pain is hidden in genes
Reawakening years of grief
Unable to ask for the means
That will bring about the right relief
But if this is what trauma can do
Where does it leave us now?
Many generations working to undo
The cycle of hurt.

Many families in North America can trace back just a few generations to some type of piercing trauma. And I wonder to what extent the effects of that trauma linger in our families, our identities, and our choices.

Grandpa was a child when Japanese Canadians were interned in Canada. Given little time to pack their things and then being forced to move inland, the west coast Japanese Canadians were subject to poor conditions alongside prevailing biases against Japanese folks during World War II. Without a doubt there is lingering trauma in the Japanese Canadian community. These Canadian citizens, targeted based on race, had no control over their lives, their property, and their possessions. Now scattered throughout Canada, this community and these people would have had to integrate to find jobs and rebuild their lives. Inevitably, many of them lost touch with their Japanese identities. Without the means and the population to establish their culture within the community, people like my grandparents likely opted for security and comfort by fitting in and doing what they needed to do to survive.

I wonder if my dad's demeanour, his silence, and his unemotional front were partly a product of generational trauma. His community had to learn to be quiet, do as they were told, and fit in to survive; much like many visible minorities who learned to keep their culture to themselves and integrate into the local culture to be successful. Maybe Dad's silence was in part a product of all these things and in part the emphasis in Japanese culture to "save face." Maybe it was this, coupled with racism and stigma around mental health, that made him feel powerless and unable to speak. And although I'll never be able to know, theorizing and finding ways to reduce these harms are undoubtedly great ways to help others, and I think that's the goal. So, as this shows, mental health needs to be understood through lenses of intersectionality because the conversations are full of nuance, they are ugly, but necessary, and I hope that "Where We Are Now" can help to make this point.

MOTORCYCLE LOVE STORY

It was a motorcycle love story
how can you be sad
romance or not,
that cycle isn't bad.

He picked her up
and burned her thighs
but she couldn't imagine
what a surprise,
their life would be.

The garage was full
of two-wheeled vehicles
and smiles beaming
on highways screaming,
how lovely life could be.

Never a worry
because life is short
enjoy it or not
when you're a good sport,
so happy we should be.

Our best memories
on leather backs
where she found love
and a place to relax,
as content as she could be.

But memories aren't stained
and there's a lot to be gained
from the mourning and glory,
of this motorcycle love story.

Mom always took the opportunity to ride a new bike; we all knew she had a tenacious love for motorbikes. I was told that when she was young, she would try to jump ditches on her dad's dirt bike, and she would regularly offer to take her friends for rides. It's no surprise that when she met my dad, she didn't hesitate to jump on the back of his bike and go for a ride. And despite burning her legs on the sides of the bike, that's where their romance started. What a perfect first date for a couple of motorbike lovers. Throughout their life together, many different toys and vehicles could be found in their garage, but the ones that Mom never complained about were the motorbikes. At one point, we had two bright red crotch rockets, two maxi scooters, and a dirt bike scattered among the garages. Dad must have known that Mom was the one when she encouraged him to bring home these types of toys. Their love for two-wheels extended beyond date night to weekend trips and rides around town with Sam and me on the pillions.

After Dad passed away, Mom sold most of the bikes but kept her own. She made sure her bike was insured and tuned up as soon as spring rolled around. I always thought that it was pretty cool that my mom would ride around town on her red ninja, and I love that she demonstrated the importance of keeping true to yourself and the things that you love no matter what was going on in your life. It was definitely therapeutic for Mom. Sometimes she would leave the house in a bit of a mood, but she always came back with a huge smile. It was no surprise that when she met a friend who worked with motorbikes, she took the opportunity to test ride a brand-new bike. But this time would be different.

Mom was with Sam at a volleyball tournament six hours from home. She took the opportunity with some of the other parents to go and test ride the new bikes. She was so excited she posted on Instagram and sent me photos along the way. But it didn't go as intended, and she never returned to the tournament. Sam was now alone at this tournament six hours north of home. She had to get a hold of me, and we figured out how she and I were going to get back to Lethbridge. I was able to catch a flight, and a family friend drove Sam in Mom's car south, picking me up along the way. And when we got home, it was just us, and we sat there, neither of us knowing what to say.

But it was a motorcycle love story, and I wouldn't have it any other way. Even though our time together was cut short, I am left with some of the best memories of amazing parents and a fun, loving, and happy family. I couldn't make myself angry at Mom or at Dad for their choices. But many other people were angry. They were angry at Mom for getting on the motorbike, and to each their own, but once you see it in the context of her life, it was no surprise that she would choose to get on that bike. Here I want to note that despite common beliefs, anger is not a necessary stage of grief—that concept is a myth, and I think a harmful one at that—rather whatever natural response your grief embodies is valid; it just doesn't have to be anger, though it might be. I say this because I have been rubbed the wrong way hearing about other people's anger toward Mom and Dad, and because some people assumed that others, like me, felt the same way. But I wasn't angry; I was just sad. Of course, I would have wanted more time and more memories, but there are things that we cannot control, and that is just the way it is. Regardless, I would have eventually lost Mom and Dad; yes, it would have been nice for them to see Sam graduate, to meet partners, to be grandparents, and all the rest, but I can't be mad. Their choices are not things that I am in any position to criticize. How can I be angry when they gave me such an incredible life? Sam and I were loved unconditionally; we were given opportunities; we travelled; we learned sports; we were given education; we formed our own identities; we were independent; and we were supported. I am beyond grateful to have had these two beautiful people in my life for as long as I did. But I found myself very angry at a variety of other things. I was angry at how people treated my mom and my sister. At how people would talk about suicide and mental health. I am angry that we have created systems that don't care about mental health or about grief, and that leaves those without similar privileges behind.

I am beyond grateful and lucky that Mom gave us so much, and so many things that we would now need. She had already taught us how to grieve, how to take care of ourselves, and how to put ourselves first. She gave us independence, a voice, an opinion, and lead by example. Mom and Dad didn't stop living their lives and being themselves when they had babies. When I was two months old, they took me to Maui so that they could vacation and, likely, windsurf. They taught us to adapt, to find things we loved, to be true to who we are, and to work on ourselves. They had prepared us for this— not that they knew that *this* is what we were preparing for. When we were young, Mom was adamant that because Sam and I were visibly Asian, or mixed-race women, we needed to learn to have a voice and to stand up for ourselves. She knew society would not rule in our favour. So she signed us up for speech and drama classes, ensuring that we would be confident and independent even at young ages. But little did she know that these lessons, and her efforts to ensure we could battle marginalization, would be the reason we have continued on living happy lives despite mass amounts of grief and trauma. I've been asked many times how I have been able to overcome the adversities that arose from my parents' deaths, and I must attribute it to these amazing parents, especially my incredible mom. I probably wouldn't have learned how to make myself happy or hurdle barriers if Mom had been different, if she hadn't worried about giving Sam and me confidence, if she hadn't chosen to prioritize herself when she needed to, if she hadn't allowed herself to continue loving motorbikes and enjoy the thrill of riding. It is these traits that taught me how to be resilient, how to continue on, and how to cope with some of the hardest parts of life. I learned from Mom's example how to continue on.

WELCOME PT.2

Welcome, again, to the community
of grievers.

You know the walls are littered with images
of those we miss,
and the memories that remain.
Where once before you've already
had to meet me.
This time the air is warmer,
but the drafts are colder,
the highs will hurt,
while the lows allow you to breathe.
And from piece to piece
you'll trek a familiar path
until you find what you need.

You may know you're not alone
roaming the gallery with the others,
this endlessly growing community
that you know all too well is reality.
Alongside those you resonate with,
those you can walk with silently,
you'll try to take two moments to enjoy,
the thoughts of your own company.
Looking at the murals around the room
you're beginning to really see me,
but it's going to be different this time around,
because grieving is never easy.

Although you never left the space
it feels different with what has just happened.
These rooms echo pains of the past
while showing you new emotions.
And while you're prepared for me
to knock you down
I'll instead steal your air.
But the community should give you
love, comfort, and care,
space to breathe,
room to speak,
validating how you're feeling.

So, welcome to the community,
of grievers.

So here we were again, at the doors of this community. Not that we ever left, but suddenly our chairs fell from beneath us, and we needed to establish new spots, navigating different situations on the way. Grief was going to be different this time; we already knew it. Because now our grief was accompanied by inherited responsibilities of a parent, professional, and homeowner. New baggage to carry with us as we traversed through the community. This time we wouldn't be able to take the time for ourselves that Mom had given to us after Dad died, and we wouldn't be able to return to a somewhat normal life. We now had a house, vehicles, legal obligations, financial worry, and so many little things to think about. All those things that we call adulting were now the responsibilities of sixteen- and eighteen-year-old women, along with unnecessarily complicated estate, trust, and legal elements. Different obstacles would arise because when Dad died, we still had Mom, and Mom filled the roles that Dad once had. Before we had to adjust to life with a single parent, but now we had to adjust to a life without parents, as adults, when really, we were just children. Being five years older than when we lost Dad meant that we had formed different types of relationships, beyond dependency, with Mom. We would be losing the friend, the parent, the cheerleader, the mentor, the teacher, the security guard, all of these different things that she was to us. And this made grief feel different because I had now begun planning my life, where many of my plans were tied to these relationships with Mom.

Entering the community this time was different because I think that many of my friends, being so close to my mom, also joined when she died. Though some of us have never spoken about it, I can tell in conversations that they get it, and many are happy to be an ear or a hand when I need it.

However, I often worry about my friends, about how grief has affected them, and whether they have found their way in this community.

~

Losing Mom, I was more prepared for grief. I was familiar with the grief community, so I knew where and how to find the support I would need. Even if I never did, knowing that it was there, that people would help if I asked, gave me the comfort and support that I often felt I needed. I also turned to the community to learn about grief; I found myself scanning various blogs, stumbling across Instagram accounts, and listening to podcasts to hear how others dealt with their life-altering losses and the many hurdles that arose. I found these online sources of information incredibly helpful and comforting; it's something I wish I had when my dad died.

DEFEATED

Because I wasn't there the second you needed it,
take me back to that hour.

You never should have sat there alone,
why didn't I know.

Your voice was silent in my pocket,
the screen silently illuminating.

My world was spinning, as yours had stopped,
realities I wish I could change.

Because the saddest part of this whole story,
is the time you had to be alone.

And the sting you feel each time you want them,
on the other end of the phone.

Calling—calling—calling,
but I could never hear you.

Notifications never more urgent,
peacefully occurring.

Because it was a deafening moment,
seeing the echoes of your voice.

Knowing instantly what words,
were creating my concern.

There is nothing I wouldn't do,
to take away that hour.

To take away all your pain,
and stop the messages from happening.

You should never have to sit alone calling out to me.
You should never have to sit alone calling out for nobody.

When Mom's accident happened, I was working in Vancouver. And as a (somewhat) responsible employee, I kept my phone on silent in my pocket. But when I took a second to look at my phone, the countless messages and calls from my sister conjured instant regret. My heart sank into the pit of my stomach and the world around me halted. I knew this meant something awful. I clicked the call back button, ran out of the building, and with just three words from my sister's lips it became real. I cried, probably screamed; I had no idea what to do. On the other end of the line police confirmed what Sam had said as my body went numb. It was hard to stand up; it was hard to breathe, and tears flew off my face. Now what?

Sam was in Edmonton, six hours away from our home in Lethbridge. She and Mom had been at a volleyball tournament for the weekend, and now Sam was left there alone. A parent of one of the players on Sam's team offered to drive her back home, so I just needed to find a way to her. All I wanted was to see my sister, to be in our home, and to undo it all, as soon as I possibly could. I ran back inside the building, whispering between tears to my boss what had happened. Thankfully, there was an airport across the road from where I was working, and one of my boss's friends ran over to check the upcoming flights. He found out that there was a flight to Calgary that had just began boarding, so he ran back to collect me. Like the speed of light, I grabbed my things, said my goodbyes, and bought my ticket home. Before boarding the flight, I made some calls and with help from family arranged a ride to a location where I could wait for the friend driving with Sam to collect me. And as though this all happened in a matter of moments, I went from being on the phone with Sam to beside her in the car, making our way home. I was so lucky to be working right beside an airport and for all the help that everyone offered. I was hardly able to think straight, barely able to keep myself standing, but it all worked out because everyone was so quick to work together. Oh boy, does it give me stress, though, just to remember those few hours. The amount of emotion, anxiety, and trauma that the day caused everyone I cannot put to words, but the saddest part for me is how long it took to look at my phone.

Sam was all alone; the police separated her from her friends to tell her the news, and all she could do was wait to get in contact with me. She was fully alone, her only caregiver, guardian, the person whom she spent her days with was now gone. I can't imagine being in her shoes, how she would have felt, or what she would have thought. She is the most incredible person I know, and that I am so lucky to know. She has been dealt a hand that she plays with grace, despite the many cards working against her. This poem is not only an apology to Sam, but also my attempt to express the amount of love and admiration I have for every aspect of her.

TRAUMA CALLED

Please don't text me more than once
    or worry will buzz within me
Try to answer as soon as I call
    or fear will ring throughout me
Don't bother with edits, undoing, or deletes
    or it'll find signal in my dream

Now I can't help but skip beats and breaths
    when notifications grow restless
When screens are layered with words from you
    I instantly regret the moon
And even after I clear the messages
    my mind calls out in distress

So now I see the screen in my sleep
    and panic surges with every beep
Because whenever my phone looks like it did that day
    fear spams all of my ability
And my guilt illuminates with every text
    why did it take me so long to check

I am so sorry I made you wait
    alone in the bathroom stall
I am so sorry I didn't answer your first fucking call

There are lasting effects of trauma and guilt that can go unnoticed while we are grieving. We may be quick to associate all the feelings that we have throughout a loss with grief, but that is just not always the case. I grew up and often neglected the nuance that should fill conversations about minds and emotions, thinking that there was one specific cause for how I was feeling. But that's never the case. Every part of your life weighs into who you are and the choices that you make. I wish I had understood this sooner because I had attributed so many of my thoughts and emotions to grief and grief alone. But now I have come to realize that there was actually a lot of trauma associated with the loss of my mom playing into my thoughts and emotions.

It wasn't until a year after Mom died that I realized how the events of that day affected me and especially how it affected my relationship with my phone. I wish that I could have seen Sam's messages earlier or answered the first time she called, not only to take away the unimaginable feelings she would have had, but to change the way I now treat my phone. Feelings of grief now flood my senses when I see many notifications. Flashbacks to the trauma of that day, the phone call I had with Sam, and the calls that I had to make. The heartbreak, shock, and anxiety that I had that day reincarnates whenever I forget to mute a group chat.

~

I never identified the anxiety that I was having with trauma. For a long time I was hesitant to use that word because I didn't want to invalidate worse trauma—oh, where to begin with this ... First, I have always been the person to gaslight myself, to compare people, compare situations, and I really didn't see anything wrong with that. But it began to hurt me. I never felt validated or content with myself because people have it worse, and people have it better. I would tell myself what I thought were affirmations and motivations, but after a while those "you're too tough to cry, too strong to break-down" comments broke me down. I never gave myself the space I needed to breathe, grieve, and understand what happened. Even reading some of my early poems (that, for good reason, I did not include in this book) shocks me; it shocks me at how unaware I was of how harmful these comments were and how they were at the root of so many of the issues that I was having. I was reactive, highly sensitive, angry, and I didn't think it was something I could change. But I learned the hard way, after many breakdowns, that I didn't need to be so hard on myself, I didn't need to be perfect. I just needed to learn how to grasp my, at the time, feral emotions. Although I am still working on it, I have gradually learned to accept my grief, my trauma, the hardest parts of my life, and how they influence me every day. Slowly, I am becoming stronger, not in the way that I understood strength before, but in the way that I am more secure in myself and who I am becoming. I have no doubt that many young grievers are in the same boat, and if you are, I want you to know how incredible it is that you are on this journey. You must be totally badass to be taking the time to work through this trauma because it's often not fun, unimaginably difficult, and painstakingly slow. I hope that, in the long run, you become everything that you want and more.

~

Ultimately, writing this poem helped me to see my trauma as trauma, a hard first step toward a healthier life. Now, things are getting better with my phone, my guilt, and my grief. Not because it's forgotten, but because it's been embraced. It's a part of me—likely always will be—and it's something I am learning to manage (and it's okay if I don't fully).

TODAY I LEARN, SO TOMORROW WE GROW

She was sixteen
Excited for life
Until life took her
She was recovering
Finally understanding
But now she had to begin again
Already independent
Stronger than she should have to be
But strength doesn't give you the cure
And no one gives her due credit
No one knows her pain
As she has learned to feel alone
"We helped" they say
As they go about their day
Forgetting what is needed to get through hers
Too much to do
No one to talk to
But she should do it another way
How does she live
So much hatred
Yet keeping things so positive
Hurting silently
Doing as she must
Excited for what
At just sixteen

Without a doubt, my sister is incredible, inspiring, and fascinating. The narrative that she lives is one that few would be able to understand. She was in Grade 11, finally finding her footing after enduring the painful loss of her dad, and suddenly, life as she knew it crumbled. She was with Mom every day, that relationship making up such a big part of her life. And now it was gone, along with the support, care, and love that her parents would have provided for the years to come. Every aspect of how she went about her life and how she thought about life was now changed. At just sixteen, she was without parents, grieving, a product of trauma, and lost as to what would be next.

I failed to empathize with her situation after Mom died. I expected her to act as I did, but the two years that separated us gave us quite different experiences. I wanted to move quickly, get everything set up and automated so that we could make the year seem as normal as our situation would allow. But moving quickly meant many meetings and making decisions on things we had never thought about before. I was confident in my choices, but consequently they might have overshadowed hers. Though she asked for more time or wanted to table certain questions I would ask, out of my own desires, I pushed her beyond her comfort and wishes. I used her strength against her and made analogies where there were none. All this invalidated the severity of her situation and made our venture toward normalcy harder. What we had experienced was in no way the same. I had two more years with these wonderful people. I had a parent at my graduation who also helped me begin university. Sam would need to provide herself with more support through each of these events, which would be coupled with her lingering grief. How she continues to wake up and go about her day is inspirational. Her mindset, attitude, and thoughts demonstrated a maturity and elegance beyond her years, but this same maturity would rob her of youthful memories.

My realization that I was so inconsiderate has been my greatest lesson of empathy. Though our situations were similar, they were in no way the same. Though I thought I knew how she was doing, I could never really know. Though I tried to do the right thing, the right thing would have been to take her perspective into greater consideration. May this poem be my lesson to have more empathy, always.

BIKINI ON A GRAVESTONE

Why do you stop
Why do you cringe
Because of a bikini on a gravestone

Because it's a church
Because it's not the norm
But what harm is a bikini on a gravestone

Though she was happy
Symbolism should conform
When it's a bikini on a gravestone

To accept and to love her
Yet so many constraints
Bothered by her bikini on a gravestone

It's the way
It's fallen astray
The idea of a bikini on a gravestone[1]

---

1 A photo of the aforementioned columbarium plaque is on page 147

When you die, how do you want to be remembered?

Note it down somewhere to save your friends and family immense amounts of anxiety so they don't have to decide how you should be remembered. For instance, after you die there are so many options for what can be done with your body. You can be buried, cremated, cryogenically frozen, turned into a tree or a diamond, or you can donate your body to health or science. And then someone has to pick where you would be buried, stored, or planted and whether there will be an accompanying plaque, gravestone, sign, or bench. And if you don't tell anyone what you want, then your poor friends and family will have to debate and discuss what they believe is the best option for you. Please, if you haven't already, take a moment to think about what you want and note it somewhere, or with someone, to save the people you love additional pain. Unfortunately, when someone dies there is pressure to answer these questions quickly and it can be very difficult for people experiencing grief to make these decisions, especially when everyone may know you a little differently and have different opinions on what to do to honour and remember you.

When my dad died, Mom chose to have him cremated, placing some of his ashes in a columbarium with a plaque at our local cemetery. Realistically, I doubt she knew what she wanted to do or how my dad would have wanted to be handled. But it was a decision that she had to make quickly, and that weighs heavily on someone still processing the news of the death of the person they loved. Mom was wholly invested in making the right decisions when designing the plaque for Dad's spot on the columbarium. She knew that establishing a place where people could visit would be important for her own mourning as well as others. I guess that is the beauty of a cemetery. Cemeteries bring people to a place where they can set aside time and thoughts to work through whatever they need to in order to keep moving forward. Mom knew that she wanted to create a beautiful plaque that she would love and that her daughters would turn to throughout life. By letting us join her to pick out the plaque and design, she showed that she knew it was important to us. Even though we were young in the eyes of society, it was important because these were the things that we would have to remember Dad by, and these were the things that would help us move forward with grief. We decided on an etched photo of Dad windsurfing with a picture of his face, name, and the date on a plaque that would stand on a columbarium tower facing the road for anyone driving by to see; it was perfect. Mom loved it so much. She was proud of it. It was a work of art within the cemetery. It truly showed Dad's personality, his zest for adventure, and it kept the happy memories of him at the surface of our thoughts.

When Mom died, this was one of the most difficult decisions we had to make. Knowing how much Mom loved Dad's plaque, and how happy we would be when we visited it, we knew we had to do something just as beautiful for Mom. Although Mom would have preferred to donate her body to science, it wasn't a viable option at the time, so we opted for cremation. She had mentioned cremation before, and she wholly loved what she'd created for Dad, so in trying to create something equally beautiful, we started to think about what we would put on her plaque. At first, I wanted to put a photo of her on her motorbike on the plaque; she was so proud of her motorbike, and she grew up riding dirt bikes, so it would have been symbolic of her adventurous spirit and enthusiastic personality. But as lovely a thought as it was, having someone who died on a motorbike, pictured sitting on a motorbike on their memorial plaque, may have been pushing the satire of the situation a bit too far for my liking.

Ultimately, we put off creating the plaque for quite some time to make sure we thought through our choices. We were focused on thinking about how to create a plaque for Mom that would correspond to Dad's, while also giving Mom's plaque the space to show the strength and independence that it took for her to move forward after Dad's death. Their lives apart were equally as valuable as their lives together; however, Mom had many years on her own where she grew independently and triumphantly without Dad. Therefore, to represent the years they spent moulding each other, while also illustrating the time Mom spent becoming an incredible woman on her own, they needed to have separate spots, but still near each other. Now, if somehow their plaques could flow together . . . and it was this idea of flowing that gave us an idea.

It was a really nice day; I had an afternoon spare in high school, so Mom asked if I would join her and go paddleboarding at a local lake. Excitedly, I grabbed my bikini and threw the boards on the car. I had brought my GoPro this day, so we took pictures and videos paddling up and the down the lake. It was a little bit choppy, but we enjoyed the workout. That day was perfectly symbolic of the type of life that my mom lived. She was outgoing, adventurous, spontaneous, and loved to get out and do things that made her happy. Overall, it was a really happy day. So, when we were deciding on photos for the plaque, I pulled out these photos and found this one of Mom, looking back, sunglasses on (a Karen staple), paddling on the open water. Bingo. I thought it was perfect, it was the perfect expression of who she was, a symbol of all the happy memories people shared with her. And the water would look as if it flowed between the plaques of my mom and dad. But there was a catch that I originally did not bat an eye at. She was in a bikini.

So here stands a perfect example of the difference in values that can arise and cause controversy throughout human life. Is it appropriate to put Mom, in a bikini, on a columbarium, in a cemetery? Here stands my argument. A cemetery is not a place that everyone treats equally, just as grief is not something that everyone treats equally. How people choose to grieve, to mourn, and to remember their loved ones is unique to each of us. So, as it stood, I didn't believe that there would be a normative argument around what should be permissible or impermissible in a cemetery. Yet those opinions still made their way to my ears.

"It is a holy place."

Well, what makes something holy? My mom did not have a traditional, religious celebration of life or burial, and I would have never considered my dad's spot on the columbarium holy. The plot of land that we buy is owned by the city, which is also not itself a holy body. The general respect that is enforced for cemeteries is due to the nature of the place, similar to a school or a museum, not due to some aspect of sacredness (unless you may find yourself in a cemetery like a graveyard that is regulated and located by a specific church or similar). Further, people of many different religious, nonreligious, and other backgrounds can be found at a cemetery, so to try and impose certain beliefs over the types of things should and should not take place in its parameters is incredibly difficult. Though we may agree that we should do what we can to prevent harm within the bounds of the cemetery, to understand what that means for regulating forms of expression requires numerous in-depth conversations with many people about the space and the various backgrounds. For instance, where my mom and dad's plaques are located would not be some place I, for one, consider holy. Rather, I believe it is a space that represents memories, emotion, and peace (not understood in the way which is linked to the religious connotations). So, I argue that stating that a cemetery is a holy place, where things can and cannot be done based on your personal beliefs without considering the beliefs of others, is an unnecessary imposition. You can see it as a holy place, but that does not mean that I will, and that does not mean that it, in fact, is. And though I wish that no one would have to justify their choices regarding grief and death, these conversations in this book are important because they show how subjective these processes, emotions, and definitions are (and in my experiences, how traditional and dated these concepts are and continue to be). Now why is that? Why is it that so many people feel they can have an opinion about a plaque on a columbarium that has been created by those who loved them to celebrate the life and memories that they have of that person? I think that when the opinion is not because of a harm that someone feels, it may be because of traditions rooted in European religions. The traditional beliefs that expect women to be nurturing, submissive, and modest alongside the ways these religions treat life and death, are likely to be reasons why discomfort or anger arises in response to this image of Mom in a cemetery. But similar to how a large portion of our western society normatively spouts their beliefs in heaven, hell, God, and superstitions, it should be equally okay to spout other beliefs as other beliefs are just as necessary for certain people's grieving processes as yours or mine. I guess by introducing this conversation I want to emphasize the importance of being open to the beliefs of others, especially when it comes to grief and death. Religious conflicts can make things extremely difficult for grievers and for those trying to do what's best for their grief and those around them. It just makes things so much more complicated, traumatic, and heartbreaking when conflict limits people's ability to heal and remember the amazing memories of those we have loved and who have passed.

Ultimately, with minds clouded by grief, differences in opinions, and many people involved, compromise is difficult. I have struggled with it, and I will likely continue to struggle with it—but you can make grieving easier for your loved ones by making these choices ahead of time (so please do—in detail).

"IT'S MEANT TO BE"

I'm sick of it

For a reason
For a purpose
Destiny
Prophecy

I'm sick of a soul
I'm sick of forever
Fuck I would hate it

We say that life is short
But how can we imagine anything longer

For me, one of the most agitating comments after both Mom and Dad passed away was that everything would be okay because it was "meant to be." People may have said this because they were at a loss for words, but with good intentions; they were trying to offer help and reassurance. This, alongside the many platitudes that we all use, tend to be default positions that we take when we are uncomfortable, unsure, but still intend to help. However, I would argue that these platitudes are often said without much thought or consideration; they often don't feel like meaningful engagement with what's being said. I know that I am guilty of it. And saying that something "is meant to be" is a prominent trend in our current language, but I think that petitioning something like this requires thinking about what it means for the situation and the person that you are talking to. Especially if you are offering condolences, I think that they should be meaningful, with intentions to really help, and they should take into consideration the person you are addressing (otherwise what is the point?). Being considerate of the griever's thoughts, beliefs, and opinions, before offering condolences, will likely be the best way to begin providing support for them. Now, this may seem to contradict what I said previously—that it's not about what you say, but how you make them feel. I guess I don't mean for that to be understood plainly. Rather, the words do contribute to how someone feels, and at least for me, "It was meant to be" elicits feelings that are not overly positive. To me, it minimizes the situation; it doesn't account for how difficult the event is going to make someone's life, as though to say, "It's not that big of a deal" or "You will get over it." So, although what we say doesn't have to be perfect, and it won't be perfect, I would just recommend knowing who you are talking to. Being empathetic will also help you find the words and actions that can help those grieving. So, by checking in, centering the person you are helping, and being mindful of their beliefs and opinions, can help us to be better friends to grievers and to create safer spaces for grief.

I recognize that what I am going to say next is heavily influenced by my religious trauma, but I think it's important to note because these are other common platitudes that can often cause a lot of pain to grievers (I will note that I haven't spoken with many people about my relationship with religion, so I know that these well-wishes meant no harm, or pain, as others reasonably assumed I followed the religion my family pressured me into; likely greater transparency would have helped me to avoid the pain caused by these statements, but it's been more difficult to have these conversations than endure the moments of discomfort). For instance, hearing people say that my parents are now watching over me, or that I will see them again, is very difficult to hear. As someone who has walked away from these beliefs and sat through uncomfortable conversations about them, hearing these things revives the anxiety and sadness that various experiences have caused me. The reality is this will happen in various forms to many of us who are grieving and who don't align with the common conceptions of life and death within our societies. So, it's good to be prepared for these moments, but I know it hurts, and I am sorry if you have ever, or will ever, experience it.

BED

The place that we come to
That we share our strongest emotions with

When waves intrude
and currents conquer
When light hurts
and dark screams
When cramps freeze
and lungs drown
When it's the holidays
or the worst days
When you need love
or you need to give love
When you've hurt
or you're hurting
When the world is spinning and spinning and spinning
and your too dizzy to see somewhere soft to fall,

It gives me the space to breathe

"Bed" was written because of the connection that I feel, and I know my family felt, toward our beds. As odd as this sounds, it may resonate strongly with some. The bed is where, as children, we would come for the extremities of any emotion. We would crawl into a bed with parents when we were scared or hide under our own covers. We would scramble into Mom and Dad's bed on Christmas morning, filled with excitement and urgency. We would gather there to cry, to laugh, to entertain, or be entertained. This is the place where Sam and I got to be ourselves. We could cry, we could laugh, and we could talk about what to do next. It was our gathering place. Our safe place. And it has become the place where the rules of how we speak and what we speak about are weaved into the linens we lie on.

After losing Dad, I spent more time in my bed then I think I ever had. I remember lying there for hours. It was the place I would return to when things became too much or if I needed a break. It was where I was most comfortable. Not only my own bed, but Sam's bed and Mom's bed. I would find myself spending most of my time bouncing between beds, chatting, napping, and hanging out. Mom's bed, though . . . that was the place to be. Sam and I would raid her bed on the nights when we were full of energy or when we just wanted to talk. It wasn't until after my mom's passing, though, that I realized the utter importance of our beds being our safe space or even just having a safe space. When we got home after Mom died, it was the bed where we found ourselves, where we were comforted, and where we looked to comfort. It is the first place I turn to; it is the place where I feel the safest and where I prepare to organize my thoughts. It is the place that gives me strength and lets me put my guard down. Sam said to me after we moved away for university that her bed is the most important part of her home. And it all started to click for me. She was so right—for our family, our beds were the most important part of our home. It's where we shared so many amazing memories, and it's where we were comfortable being vulnerable.

When Dad died, Mom understood this. She would let Sam and me stay in our rooms and in our beds as long as we needed. She ensured no one would interrupt or bother us unless we agreed because she knew the value in having this safe space. Even though many people came to our house after Dad and Mom died, we knew it was important to keep them away from our safe spaces so that we could take a moment to get away from the people and the conversations and work through whatever thoughts we were having. Without this, I wouldn't have been able to make the decisions that I am now happy with. I would have felt weaker, more uncertain, and vulnerable wherever I went because I wouldn't have had a place that I could rely on for confidence.

All in all, if you resonate with the idea that your bed is your happy place, your sad place, or your most emotionally connected place, don't turn away from it—embrace it. Give yourself those safe spaces. Create pockets of happiness and comfort so that when things do become uncontrollable or chaotic, you know where you can turn. Then we need to make sure that we are allowing others their safe spaces as well, by realizing where we fit into other safe spaces and where we do not. It is time we make sure that everyone has safe spaces.

CAN'T HELP BUT THINK OF YOU

I pick up the phone,
but with no one to call,
a habit that shows
on the best of days
one can't help but think of you.

Curly, frail hair, bouncing
to a contagious laugh,
an unappreciated essence,
until it all became
a memory.

We miss seeing how beautifully
a woman can age.
The wet kisses and bear hugs,
a sweet smile
giving life to bad jokes.

Teaching one to be kind
by being the best example.
Celebrating the victories,
no one else could see.

Voices lingering,
lessons dawning.
With fuzzy compliments,
reminding people of you.

It wasn't until I experienced grief that I really began to understand my love and appreciation for Mom and Dad. Though it may be normal that only after we lose something we begin to realize how much it meant to us, the reality of it is kind of upsetting. There were many amazing things said about Mom after she died that I don't think she ever heard. I think she would have been ecstatic hearing the wonderful things that people thought about her. However, seeing this has made me wonder if losing access to a person is necessary to realize the value that they have in my life. Am I able to really understand the love and appreciation that I have for someone while they are still with me? I'd like to think so, but I'm starting to doubt it. Maybe that's one of the bittersweet products of grief, gaining access to your new feelings about a person, but without the ability to share them with them. Ultimately, I now know to be a better cheerleader for the people I love while I am with them. To express my love for them, to tell them what I find incredible about who they are and the joy that they bring me. As cliché as it is, once someone is gone, you can't tell them how you feel, or how they made you feel, so why not do it now? It feels as though we don't appreciate our living angels enough.

~

Something that births a plethora of emotions is the moment you pick up the phone to call the person who is now gone. A week after Mom died, I got into my car angry about a conversation I'd had, and I called her phone. It rang twice before I clicked "end." In that moment, it hit me; all the support that Mom provided was now gone, and so much of this support went unrecognized. She was always a call away, and I took advantage of that every moment I could. As I sat in my car that day, my tears of anger turned to frustration and sadness as I removed her contact from my favourites. Even years after Mom died, I found myself doing the same thing. Turning my phone on, clicking the phone app favourites, and just then realizing I couldn't call her. It was like clockwork, a habit that I couldn't break. Whenever I was excited, nervous, anxious, or thrilled I would have normally called Mom. It's been five years and it still happens, less than before, but still, every once in a while I find myself in the midst of an overwhelming emotion and have the urge to call Mom.

What I didn't realize early in my journey with grief was the number of different ways that I would be affected by no longer having Mom on the other side of my calls. Before Mom died, I talked to her on the phone nearly everyday, sometimes twice a day. There wasn't a single genre of conversation that we would shy from. Because of this, Mom was a huge source of validation and support for me. I would run all my ideas and decisions by her, whether I was looking for an opinion or just the opportunity to say it out loud. And even if Mom wasn't overly fond of the idea, she always gave me confidence in my choices and supported the paths that I chose. Surprisingly, I didn't feel like I lacked confidence or validation right after Mom died. Although I would have loved to hear what she wanted for her funeral and what advice she had for me that year, I was confident in my decisions; it was as though I could hear her saying "good idea," "good job," and "you've got it." For many years, for most of my decisions, I could hear her echoes of support. I continued to feel empowered and supported by her as I followed along the various paths that her and I discussed at length. But once I reached a certain bend in the road my confidence began to deteriorate. New opportunities laid in front of me that I had never spoken to Mom about. Decisions like whether I should get a dog, where I should go to law school, or if I should publish a damn book. Suddenly, I couldn't hear Mom's familiar lines of support, the ones that had given me the extra confidence that I needed for decisions before. No kidding. Mom had never told me to get a dog—but I longed to hear her say it. Unfortunately, this feeling, this longing has been a newer effect of Mom's death in my life. For years, I didn't have to make decisions where I couldn't hear her voice or remember a conversation that we had had about it. And even now, years after her death, I still draw from the validation and support she had given me for certain choices. But when new situations arise, I can't help but feel a little less certain in my choices, upset that I won't be able to know what she would think and saddened because it makes me really miss her.

OH

You'll love this new movie,
laughing hysterically,
embarrassing me –
oh

She's so sweet and cuddly,
smart and fluffy,
you'll love her little –
oh

That restaurant is coming,
it says it'll be open soon,
we should –
oh

I can't believe it,
I've been accepted,
now you'll –
oh

This thing is wonderful,
so soft and hydrating,
you need to try –
oh

He's the best part of my day,
caring and kind of dreamy,
I wonder if you'll like –
oh

Oh my gosh look at the view,
it seems too good to be true,
do you think I should –
oh

When I went to the movies with friends shortly after my mom passed away, I looked up at the billboard outside the movie theatre and thought, ***Ooo, Mom would love this***. And in that same moment, my heart sank as the air in my lungs solidified. This was one of the first moments when I realized all of the normal things she would miss out on. I realized that not only was I going to miss watching these movies with her, but, tragically, she would no longer be able see any of Anne Hathaway's endeavours. The thought that I'd now watch these without her, unable to tell her about them, and knowing full well that Mom would have loved them, makes me teary-eyed for reasons that I still cannot fully grasp. In part, it must be because I just want to tell her about them, and I want to share these experiences with her . . . and specifically her. But it also makes me wish that she would have had more opportunities, that she could have finished getting her pilot's licence or travelled more. Although looking at a billboard is a seemingly mundane event, it caused me such a flurry of emotions and thoughts, and honestly, I needed to shield myself from those types of exposures for quite a while after Mom died.

On another note, whenever there were big changes or events in my life, the first thing I always did was talk to Mom or Dad. I wanted to know what they would say and how they would react. After they died, this did not change, and even now I find myself thinking about what they would say, or how they would react, as though they were still here. These thoughts make my heart skip a beat twice over: first, when I realize they are gone and second, when I realize I will never know the answer. These two moments, these two instances of "oh," have been hard to accept and hard to escape.

~

Something that I wish I'd known earlier in my journey with grief is how to shield myself from things and experiences that are triggering and uncomfortable. I found that when I was in spaces where I didn't feel safe or supported, my strength began to cripple, and I would move steps backward in my healing process. Although it's normal to not be strong enough for some things—and we won't be able to protect ourselves from everything—finding ways to protect myself has been a catalyst for my growth and healing. For instance, very shortly after Mom died, I was driving and saw a motorbike, the first one since her death. I had to pull over because I soon couldn't see behind my tears, and I couldn't hold the wheel because of how badly my body was shaking. Seeing it shocked me, made me incredibly sad, and quite fearful. I began thinking about Mom's accident, and all these feelings that I wasn't prepared for began to materialize. Truly, I just wasn't ready for these parts of life—to see things that could bring about so many emotions—because I didn't yet know what a trigger was, and I barely had the time to process what had happened when I had to start interacting with the world. I was completely unprepared for this situation, though it's not at all shocking that seeing a motorbike after Mom died would be quite triggering—I just didn't know how to prepare myself for these uncomfortable situations. Instead, I gained further trauma because my reaction to seeing the motorbike interfered with my ability to drive and I worried about whether it would continue to happen.

Many grievers will understand this type of trauma, the trauma brought about by a genuine feeling of fear toward the world and toward the things that will cause your mind and body to react in ways you'd never be able to predict. Grievers need time to reintegrate, to process what has happened, and to think about these questions on their own time. And although many things will still be triggering, and we will still have these experiences, finding ways to protect ourselves from them— whether that be with time or resources—will be crucial for our healing and for our interactions with the world once again. One way that I prepare myself for triggers is through controlled conversations in comfortable environments. By speaking with friends, family, or mental health professionals in spaces where I feel comfortable setting boundaries and directing the conversation, I have been able to introduce topics or thoughts that are triggering, but in ways that allow me to become comfortable with them. For instance, I began to unlearn the fear and anxiety that I had associated with motorbikes by talking about it, and hearing others talk about it, in a space where I felt completely comfortable. Having agency in those conversations was essential because it allowed me to pause or reroute the conversation before I began to associate further negativity with the topic. But it took many comfortable discussions about motorbikes for me to transform the negative feelings into ones that I could manage. But by no means am I cured of this trauma, rather, my ability to manage this trauma will be something I have to continue working on and keeping in check so that it doesn't one day reappear.

~

Another thought that I had while writing "Oh" was about the complicated feelings that I have towards Lethbridge, the city that Sam and I were born and raised in. No matter how excited I am to be back in Lethbridge, as I drive into the city the negative feelings that overwhelm me far exceed the positive. I feel like I can't catch my breath, even as I look out the window to such familiar places. I feel sharp pains of unwanted memories that surface with sudden reminders.

I try to distract myself, but it's hard not to feel the same twists and turns in the road that once had taken me home, to a family, with Mom and Dad and dinner on the table. Oh boy, do I miss coming home to those cooked dinners. Even the smell of that city will bring about memories buried deep in my mind, reminding me of what I once had. This city, my "home," seems to be filled trauma and triggers. It is hard to understand how the place that was once my most safe space, has become synonymous with full body anxiety and immense heartbreak.

And then, from these feeling and thoughts arrive the difficult question: Where is home? To which I need to answer for myself—what is home? Especially having lived away from Lethbridge for many years now, and without parents, I really struggle to answer this question. Truly, where I feel the most at home is in Toronto, in my condo with my dog and when Sam is visiting. But sometimes people ask, "Where is home?" because they want to know where someone grew up, or where their parents live, or to know where that person feels the most comfortable. But when where you grew up is triggering, it's hard to call it home. And when someone wants to know where a parentless person's parents live, they are faced with a conversation that they may not want to partake in. And although it seems harmless to ask about home, it can be quite hard for those who don't have one that is easily identifiable.

SYMPATHY CARDS

Words cannot express
My heart aches
She will be fondly remembered
The most caring, loving, dedicated individual
Your mom was a very special person
A character
Her zest for life
Her humour
Her love for you both
carried her on
She could light up a room
and I'm a better person
because of her
A force of life
that would make my day better
even if it was already
a great day
I wish just once, you could see how she would smile
when she would talk about you both
Unlike any other
She left her mark on this world
and will surround you
as you do the same

This poem is composed of some of the most beautiful notes we found in the hundreds of sympathy cards we received after Mom died. These comments made me feel light, fuzzy, and warm, despite the dismal ambience filling the envelopes. Reading these comments from friends, strangers, and family helps me to remember my mom and the beautiful woman she was for so many people. She always urged us to "kill others with kindness," and the many notes that we received proved that she truly lived by that motto. As such, this poem has become a reminder of the woman I aspire to be, of the lessons she taught me, and of the immense joy kindness can bring others.

~

Writing sympathy cards and offering condolences can be quite daunting . . . we want to sympathize, but we don't want to invalidate; we want to help, but we may not know how to; we try to be kind and warm, but often we are also grieving. Hopefully reading and thinking about these topics can give us greater insights so that we become more comfortable writing and talking about loss and grief in ways that are comfortable and empathetic. And although, as previous discourse has revealed, there aren't right or wrong things to write in a card, the intentions behind the words can be the most impactful for those who are hurting. Whether it be about how you feel, a story, an intention, or an affirmation, helping people feel supported and validated can lighten a heavy heart. But I will add that sending cards is also not necessary. As lovely as these cards are, I can't remember exactly who said what—just how some notes made me feel. So, if you don't think you can write anything that will help, don't feel socially pressured to do so. There are many ways to show your support and empathy that don't require words and paper. Some of the things that I most appreciated were delivered meals, people coming to do yard work or offering to clean, grabbing groceries, and helping to organize my schedule. These types of things will not only lift heavy hearts, and help grievers take more time for themselves, but they also give grievers greater confidence in the support that they have.

~

One of the most incredible sympathy gifts I have ever received was from a long-time friend of my dad. This guy took the time to sit down and write out so many beautiful stories he had about my dad from when they were young. From playing arcade games to moments shared with their families, these stories gave me glimpses into my dad's life that I would have never known. These stories have also helped me answer questions about my dad that, only years after his death, I'd begun to think about. By being able to sit down and read these stories, I have been able to find time to think about Dad, to think about the person he was and how he continues to influence me. Sometimes it is so difficult to find the time to reflect, to sit with your grief, and remember these beautiful people that you continue to share so much with. Mysteriously, just thinking about Mom or Dad, talking about them, or hearing other people talk about them makes me so incredibly happy. Speaking and thinking about them brings a type of joy that is hard to describe, where I can keep feelings of longing at the door and welcome revived happiness.

WHY ARE YOU PULLING THE RUG?

Pull the rug out from beneath your own feet
and ask how you fell.
Tug quicker,
fall harder.
Around the world the rug shifts
and from behind you'll never see
your earth sneaking by,
until all you can perceive, is the irony.

Sometimes we hurt ourselves. We may not know it at first; we likely don't realize that we are when we do, and sometimes we never realize. For a large part of my journey with grief, it wasn't easy for me to take a step back, to analyze myself critically, or to receive the criticism that would help me to understand where I was hurting myself. Even though I knew it could help so much in the end, I kept my guard up, defended myself, and fought for my perspective. It's what pain and discomfort had taught me to do, a defence mechanism I extended to many parts of my life, but something I should have left at the door.

"Why Are You Pulling The Rug?" tries to depict what it looks like, for ourselves and others, when we can't see that we are hurting ourselves. An author may call this a fatal flaw, a part of the character that knowingly or unknowingly causes themselves harm. And often this is the kind of harm that grief preys on, causing us to hurt ourselves by magnifying our flaws, our pain, and the pleasure that we feel. Grief will cloud our judgment and fill us with numerous emotional or physical responses to loss, blinding our ability to see beyond what will immediately cure our pain. Mourning seems to prey on this—it preys on our inability to interpret the world differently, on needing to somehow look beyond ourselves to realize how to be happy. When grief makes you become your own worst enemy, it's a vicious cycle, one that is very difficult to escape; but with time, and by working through the chain of causation to see why it is you are causing yourself such harm, maybe that's when we can drop the rug.

~

When Dad died, I began expecting so much from my mom. She had such a grasp on everything, shielding us from pain while concealing her own. For many years, I couldn't empathize with her situation. I was so stuck in my own perspective that empathy was quite unfeasible. Maybe it was an unfortunate response to the trauma or a way to ensure I prioritize working on myself. But regardless of why I was that way, I wasn't a great daughter as a result. I invalidated so much of Mom's pain, expecting and asking more from her then she could give because "it was her job" . . . Oh my poor mom, having to deal with two angsty teenage children in a house filled with grief.

Though Mom and I had a few unforgettable arguments...one stands out because it helped me to realize exactly what this poem is trying to convey. Mom had forgot to pick me up from volleyball practice many times at this point, and I was now immensely embarrassed, impatient, and likely filled with hormonal emotions. I sat in the car and began to yell at Mom, telling her how terrible a parent she was, that none of my friends' parents would forget to pick them up, and I began questioning her love for me. In response, Mom did not hesitate to turn the volume up and explain herself. Between Sam and me, Mom had to pick us up and drop us off at different locations six times a day. Practice times and locations would change, and she could barely keep our schedules straight. She had no help, no time, but wanted us to continue doing all the activities that we had done before Dad died. She was trying her best to be both parents, everywhere at any given time, while finding the little time she had to take care of herself—we both began to cry. Before this argument, I hadn't realized the ways that grief was materializing for Mom. And I didn't the realize the ways that we both felt pressure because of grief and because of our new situations; for me it was to be picked up on time like the other kids, to not be seen as different, and for Mom, it was to still give us the lives we would have had before Dad died, to not be seen as different.

To this day, I feel sick to my stomach when waves of grief take me to the places in my memories that I have not yet visited with new eyes. The ones where my lack of perspective was the barrier to my own happiness. Where I didn't account for grief, so it didn't account for me. And where I hurt the people around me because I was not yet able step into their shoes.

~

While writing "Why Are You Pulling the Rug?" my relationship with confidence was at the forefront of my mind. As I mentioned earlier, though confidence was helpful in getting me to where I am today, it has also been a huge pain point throughout much of my life. So confident in my ability to be resilient, I was gaslighting myself, never giving myself the chance to heal. So sure about how things should be done, I invalidated my friends' and family's feelings on numerous occasions. This confidence, though it had become my shield and protection from hurt in the world, was also deeply hurting myself and people around me. I had to learn, and I am still learning, how to balance this trait. But grief made this realization harder, as it clouded my thoughts and told me that confidence—and narcissism—was necessary to heal and move forward. I saw much of my success as a product of this overconfidence, which was only seen as success because of my overconfidence. Here I was pulling the rug out from beneath my feet, unable to really heal and support the people around me. So stuck in that perspective, it took me falling on my face and realizing the hurt that I had caused Sam to start to change. I had to relearn how she felt, through a lens that genuinely cared to support her, through a lens that, for once, wasn't thinking about myself and my opinions. Every emotion, every feeling, everything is valid. Everything you need and everything you want, we will work to achieve. Because there are reasons behind everything, and we need to address and accept each part of it to heal and become healthier. Realizing this, I began to let myself feel genuinely sad. I stopped letting my inner voice tell me that I am too tough to be sad or that there are better things to do. And as I began to let go of those thoughts, my anger and my anxiety reduced; I finally felt heard by myself—how odd. I was finally able to let go of relationships that I knew weren't good for me, and I let go of the things that made me feel invalidated. During this journey of becoming better for myself, I think I've become better for everyone else. But it took the hard realization that I was pulling the rug.

BUT WE ARE ALL JUST THE SAME

I'm overwhelmed
sunshine reaching the line
so close to breaking dawn.
How could you know
a sinking ship scrambling for vests
propped on a boat not yours.
Invalidated, under appreciated
stalking basic needs on safari lands
but just an elephant shrew.
Surely related to
parrots repeating the honest words
leaving no breath for the wolf to cry.
Happy for you though hardly with you
degrees scattered along the wall
never reflecting your own temperature.
Making others feel small
a peacock with feathers spread
turning a blind eye to words of paradise.
Incompatible feelings
too coy to erect sympathy
when glass needs to shatter to see through.

Maybe we were running with hyenas
lions beneath a costume
unable to claim our pride
silent amongst their laughter
never left to heal
taken advantage of for strength
crying louder with their own pain
our empathy saying,
we are all just the same.

We aren't all the same. Though things might be similar, no two situations are ever identical. However, it's often hard to avoid analogies; it's hard to treat everything as novel or as unique in the world that we have created. But there are just so many pieces playing with different forces. So much nuance in every situation that we will likely never be able to understand. Though our grief is unique, grievers find their way within the limited options available, the limited spaces that allow them to grieve. It's no wonder that many grievers find themselves becoming people they never wanted to be. As though we have created spaces for specific kinds and not for all, we are surrounded by barriers that don't allow us to heal in ways that work for us. I think realizing this—that my emotions and actions are extremely complex so what works for others won't necessarily work for me—has helped me tremendously with my grief. It's shown me that I need to create my own spaces, that I need to find ways past barriers, and that I will forever be learning about the complex parts of my grief.

~

Understandably, when it comes to young people and grief, there is plenty of fear and many questions about how to help them or how to prepare them. Though no advice will be perfect or work for every person, one of the things that helped me battle and befriend grief the most was a co-curricular activity we called "Speech and Drama." I started taking these classes in kindergarten, and soon, I began training to "act the part," to empathize with the character, to understand how the piece came to be, and to be highly aware of nonverbal communication. The things I learned from Speech and Drama prepared me to navigate conversations and present myself the way I'd like. By learning about the individuality of characters, I began to question my own. By learning about character development, I began to realize the need to change and grow. And by learning about the history of the characters, the authors, and the pieces, I learned the role that the past plays and the importance of understanding it to move forward. But one of the most valuable lessons it taught me was to think independently about all of these things. As my lovely instructor would question me about the use of language, punctuation, and the tone of different pieces, I had to interpret the piece and understand the emotions it was trying to convey or that I would want it to convey. At the time, I didn't know that learning to think independently and confidently about these pieces would become such essential tools for understanding the subjective aspects of my life, or for the grief I would later feel. But when we are privy to parts of the world that we can only individually explain and work through, without confidence in ourselves and our thoughts, how would we be able to communicate our hurt, wants, and needs? As it stands, the only person that can really know about your thoughts, feelings, and emotions is you. And if you aren't able to understand them, to believe them, or to communicate them, how will anyone know how to help you? Learning to think independently about individuality, character development, the role that history plays, and having confidence in those thoughts, have been my tools to understand and narrate the grief in my life. Though I was sometimes reluctant to study for my Speech and Drama lessons, I know they were some of the most important lessons that I could have had because they prepared me for the hardest parts of my life ahead.

~

Another piece that I wanted this poem to symbolize is how important it is to treat young grievers as aware and smart people. We may tend to discredit or brush aside the questions and complaints of those younger than us, but that's when we have the opportunity to help them the most. They may lack experiential education, but they also lack the imprinting of some unhelpful habits and societal pressures. Like a sponge, they are learning so much, but also like a sponge they are fragile, lacking the resources and experiences to protect themselves from hurt. And much of this extends to people of all ages. We all think and are shaped by what we say and how we say it. No matter the age, we can feel invalidated; we can be hurt; and we can hurt each other. And given that young people already face numerous changes and difficulties with understanding themselves, to help them grieve we should be especially empathetic and understanding. I have found that the struggles are scarier the younger one is because unfamiliarity is gas on a fire of fear.

I was only 13, my sister 11, when our dad died. Nonetheless, we were both highly aware of how we were being perceived . . . the narratives, judgment, and whether people were genuinely supportive. To this day, I remember the people who invalidated how I felt, who wouldn't answer my questions all because of my age, because I "would one day know better" or because I "couldn't yet understand." These people stood in stark contrast to those who would take time listening to how I felt and being open to any questions, no matter how "immature" or uninformed they were. The latter gave me confidence to continue asking questions and sharing with others how I felt, all while ensuring I needn't feel guilty for spending the time with them. The latter helped me to grieve, while the former made me feel embarrassed for it.

Luckily, my mom realized this and did what she could to respect my grieving process in a way that allowed me to be independent and grieve comfortably. Mom consistently assured Sam and me that she would love us no matter what we did, or who we became; and this created a relationship built with trust from an early age. This trust allowed us to feel safe and comfortable speaking to her about all types of things. Another thing that Mom ensured was that we felt safe, supported, and protected. She went to the extent of having locksmiths check all the doors and windows in our house, making sure to tell us they couldn't find an easy way in (I don't think this was really a worry of mine at the time, but it was nice to know—though it might have bred a bit of worry, aha). She also extended this philosophy in a way that had a huge impact in my ability to feel safe and to support myself: by allowing me to choose when I attended school. Though this option might be a fear for some parents, Mom trusted that if I felt like going to school wasn't in my best interest for that day, it was for a good reason. When the school would call to declare my absences, she would always excuse me and check in to make sure I was doing okay. This freedom helped me feel validated, helped me feel safe, and helped me avoid unpleasant situations. For instance, as a student in a Catholic school, we had to take religion classes. Many conversations spoke about death, life, and even suicide. I knew I did not need to sit in a class with someone teaching me that suicide is a sin, so Mom happily called to excuse me as I skipped out of these types of classes (and frankly I wish that many of my friends could have had the same option). And although Mom probably worried about me falling behind in junior high and high school, she knew that processing grief and learning how to support myself would help me build a happier and more successful life. By providing resources and support, Mom was able to help me build confidence and work through grief as I wanted at my school, with my friends, and within my family. To this day, I am very grateful that my mom allowed me to grieve at my own pace and return to school when I felt ready. I think that my ability to write, speak, and understand my grief to this extent is largely a product of those choices and my feelings being validated by Mom throughout my journey with grief.

RED

Red
as the theory suggests.
Anger is a part of me.
It is in front of me,
influencing me—
disorder, discomfort, distinct
depression. I try to find
my balance
but keep emerging
from dark places
needing to be embraced by light
changed into the other side
content as I feel
as it makes the most of me—
order, comfort, happiness.
I find my balance,
breathing calm.
Blue.

Much like after Dad died, when Mom passed, I began having nightmares. I would wake up shaking, sweating, and fearful about some of the most irrational things. The nightmares came frequently, multiple times a week, for months at a time. I didn't want to sleep, and I hated feeling alone at night. It was as though I were a child again, waking up just to hide, sweating under the covers until dawn broke. As my lack of sleep started bothering me throughout the day, I reached out to my counsellor. After hearing about the nightmares, she began to break down a theory for me. She explained that one way to understand emotions, feelings, and thoughts is by categorizing them as certain colours. Blue is calm, content, and serene. Red is anxious, angry, and frustrated. I had always operated best with blue emotions, but there were many red ones surrounding me at the time. I was frustrated and annoyed with the dice I'd rolled, with how I was treated, and the things people said. The people around me were also red, and how I interpreted the world came with a red hue. As simple as it is, we assumed that these nightmares were a product of too much red, and not enough blue, because once I started to avoid the reds and made an effort to be and see blue, they started to go away. It seems like I was contributing to these nightmares, just by spending too much time with and around the emotions that I was uncomfortable with. I was going to sleep sad and then waking up frustrated, I was consistently in triggering situations and all along I thought I was invincible or that I would be unaffected by it all. But it was a cycle that I might not have escaped without help, without becoming mindful of myself and the things happening around me, and without setting boundaries to limit the red surrounding me. Even though this theory takes a very complex situation and explains it simply, this simplicity was what I needed to take a step back and learn how I could help myself.

GRIEF, A STORY TO MY PARTNER

The day will be sunny
with shio ramen and beautiful views,
but I'll struggle to find my smile.

Holidays will bring colourful lights
fun drinks and costume parties,
but tears will find my eyes.

Excited in one moment
winded the next,
working to find my breath.

And you'll hold my hand
dry my eyes,
asking questions to find out why.

To my significant other
I'm sorry it takes me awhile to explain,
awhile to find the words.

I worry about the weight
you'll wear with my pain,
if you find yourself dark on the lightest of days.

Though I wish you could know more than just what I say
these are shoes I never want you to step into,
and experiences I'll forever try to keep away from you.

Because when you're my peace
my hope, my safety, and my dream,
I fear hurt will taint these wonderful things.
But each time you've pulled back the cover

and carried my vulnerability in your arms,
we find ourselves growing closer together.

So to my significant other
I'm sorry about the pill you take for loving me,
but thank you for being all the comfort I need.

Losing friends and family at young ages brings with it a number of difficult conversations. But the conversations that I continue to struggle with are those with partners about my parents. It's already a challenge to understand grief, your own, and that of others, so trying to explain it to someone who is so keen to know but won't easily understand leaves us in a pickle. I've been in relationships where my partner wants to help, tries to help, but I can't communicate how I am feeling. Or where my partner sees how grief influences me and wants to understand more, but I almost don't want to explain it to them. I find it incredibly difficult to show my pain to someone who I never want to feel pain because I worry about the hurt that it might inflict on them. Even when I know it would help us grow together and help me heal, I hesitate because I don't want them to feel how I have felt. I have also struggled with the labour of explaining how important certain parts of grief are to me. Like how I want to talk about my parents often, but also not at certain times. Or that I want my partner to know so much about Mom and Dad that it's as if they had met, and then we can imagine together how Mom and Dad would react to our lives now. And I wish my partner would know why friends say I laugh like my mom, and why certain smells, sounds, or places make me emotional. But the depth of conversation for each of these little things is so much work and requires so much time that sometimes I feel like it's not even worth dreaming of. On top of it all, I just wish that I could have one memory of you with them.

Another hurdle that has come with losing parents is the amount of emotional support that I am left wanting. Without parents checking in, to call when I'm upset, or to share the occasional meal with, leaves me with far more time to myself and needing others to fill the roles that parents once did.

That's why I'll turn to you, that's why I'll maybe ask more of you then you will of me, and why I will want to work hard to have a relationship with your family. But before we can get to this point, I'll want to stop because I don't want to hurt you. I don't want to unload my pain or go into detail about how I feel, because I know your empathy will make you feel the hurt too. Sometimes I wish my story could be different for you.

Even though we have learned that you love me for these things, it is taking time for me to unlearn the silence that is expected of grievers. And although grief brings pain into our relationship, it also brings strength, empathy, and optimism. These conversations will bring us closer; by helping us grow together, learn together, and prepare for our future heartaches together. Maybe the pain is our necessary step to building a relationship better than we ever could have imagined. But I ask just two things: let me take it slow, and try your best to listen. Some of these things I only want to say once; some of this history re-traumatizes me every time I say it. Some of the things that I want you to know are going to need hours of backstories and history to understand. Some things I will require hours to find the words for, and some things I will want to get out of the air super quick. I'm sorry that life with me is going to be like this, but I hope it helps us become happier than ever.

FIVE YEARS LATER

I've begun to heal
but I've made some mistakes.
I understand some
but my heart still breaks.
Learning everyday
what it will take for me say
it's become easier.

I built myself up
but I have many questions
I never thought to ask
while teaching your lessons.
For if I knew
the things I'd do
to learn all you'd say.

Your image persists
but it distorts and blurs
when memories are all
that remain after years.
Though stories will continue
the ones with you
teaching us be—what next?

Now that it has been five years since losing Mom, I can say more confidently—grief fucking sucks. For a multitude of reasons that can range from traumatic to hilarious, grief has shown to be quite a pain in my ass, but also something that I value deeply. And since this book has written over the last five years, reading it has helped me to remember all these feelings and see how everything has changed immensely. My thoughts have changed from when I first wrote some of these poems, and new perspectives have shaped the later ones. Some of these thoughts, though still valid, seem so different from what I believe and think now. Though I understand the mindset that framed what I used to write, it's hard to say that those ideas are still some that I identify with. Without digressing into an entire discussion about identity theory, I'll just say that the ability to change so drastically feels like a beautiful feature of dynamic identities, but one that brings with it so much confusion. Because alongside grief, this growth and these changes can also surface so much hurt. When I learned to empathize with different perspectives, I began to feel a lack of closure regarding certain situations, and I felt guilty about how I had acted. When I began learning about mental health, I realized where I had been invalidated and where I had invalidated others. When I began to understand past experiences, I felt new trauma and had to struggle with reclaiming parts of my identity. But also, when I began to understand my grief, I realized how incredible Mom was and I how lucky I was to learn about grief from her. Ultimately, these changes can be confusing because they can hurt, and they heal. And five years later, I am a different person because of grief. Now grief burns in different ways; like when I wish that I could reintroduce myself to Mom and Dad, as this person who is so different from the one that they once knew. I wish I could just see their reactions. And Sam! Oh my gosh, how

I wish that they could meet Sam. From the small person that she was at 11 years old to now, she has grown into such an intelligent and gorgeous woman whose wit—to their surprise—would have Mom and Dad cackling in just seconds.

~

The one thing that has struck me and continues to strike me, even five years later, is the longing that I feel for Mom, for her support, guidance, and lessons. There are so many things that I learned from her, that I now forget. Certain things that she used to say—I never asked what they meant. I never got to ask her how she managed having so much empathy or where she drew so much of her strength from. She knew what to say that would make me feel better, but now I forget what that was. She would say how excited she was to be a grandparent, to help us plan weddings, or to take us travelling. So many things that I was eager to learn from her, and that I was excited to experience with her, I have had to say goodbye to. I miss more than just the beautiful woman that she was, but everything that she was also going to be. So, five years later, I am left confused, longing, but still grateful. She clearly left us prepared to take on the world, but I wish I knew how she did it. As much as I can manipulate the story to fill in the blanks, I am still left longing to hear some of the answers from her.

THANK YOU

For the gift I'll never appreciate enough,
because she's the best of both of you.
For the woman, friend, and sister,
that I can love the way I loved you.
For the one that reminds me every day,
of all the fun we once had.

She's my reason to live, my reason to fight,
and my example of how to survive.
She has your smile, and has your eyes,
so you're never that far away.
She's becoming a person I wish you could meet,
inspiring in every way.

But I wish I never came to realize these things,
or it was a conversation for another day.
Because although it seems inevitable,
no one deserves this pain.
And though I'd change it for her in a second,
I'm so grateful we have each other.

So thank you sister,
thank you father,
and thank you my lovely mother.

A poem, or a letter, or maybe just a note detailing the thanks I wish I could express to Sam, Mom, and Dad. As this book takes control of this moment's narrative of my story and of my grief as a young adult, I want to recognize the immense gratitude I have for my parents and sister who have shaped my ability to produce this account and share these conversations. Without the experiences they provided, and the foundations they built for me, I fear I wouldn't be able to find joy in life the way I can now. And especially without my incredible sister, I don't think I'd be half the person I am today.

~

Finally, to everyone reading who has grieved, who is grieving, and who will grieve—you've got this. Each day you get up, each awful emotion you conquer, and each exhausting breath you take is a small victory of your own. Be proud of your victories, be proud of your strength, and give yourself the space you need to grieve.

All my love to each of you.

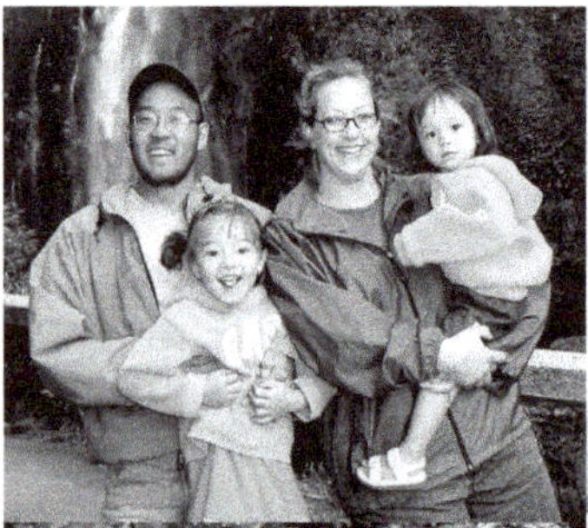
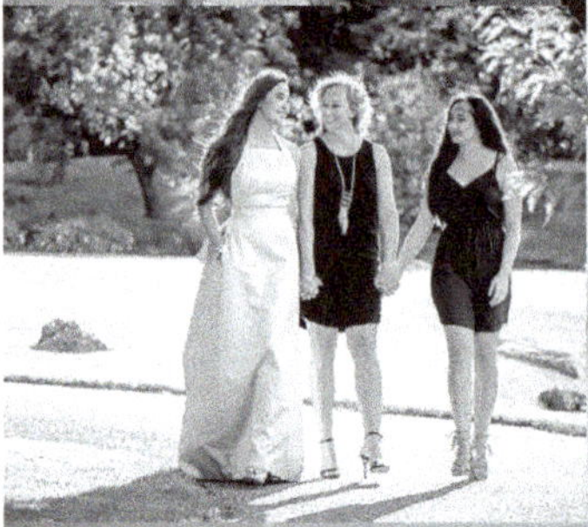
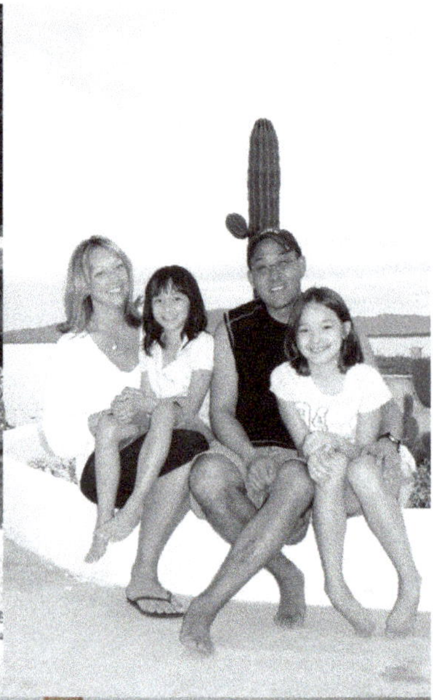
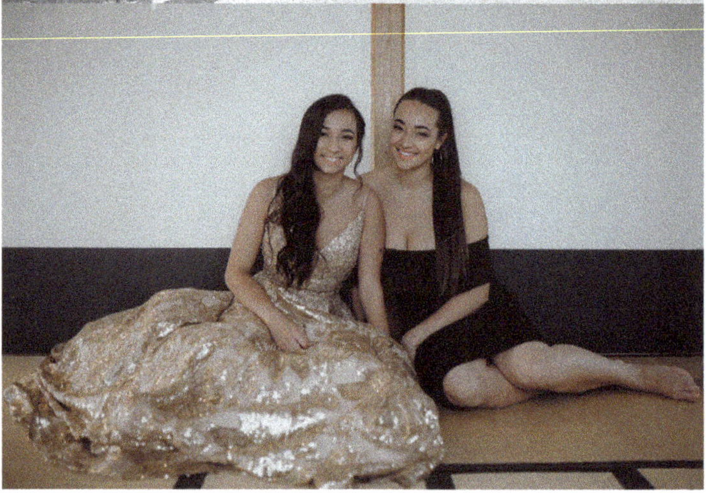

See it for yourself at Mountain View Cemetery:
1210 Scenic Dr. South - Lethbridge, AB Canada

KARENDIPITY

It is what she would have called this book
and it would have been beautiful
quirky, insightful,
and full of hope
like she was,
telling herself every day
that all would be okay
that she would find what makes her happy again
in a new, brilliant way,
never wishing her unhappiness on anyone
the one caused by loss,
confusion, misfortune
because she slowly grew to see
the value of her memories
making the most of tragedy,
letting it define the best parts of herself,
this was her philosophy
so maybe we just need
a little Karendipity.

To conclude, I am hoping to stamp the legacy of my wonderful mother into the literature that will live beyond my memories. As I've mentioned, Mom had the intention to write her own book one day, so I hope I can do her intentions justice and share pieces of what I believe she would have wanted to share with others. To be honest, I wasn't quite sure how I was going to start this ending, but coincidentally a memory was revived late one night, pointing me in the right direction.

Growing up, the word *serendipity* often left Mom's lips—a word that I never fully understood and frequently asked others to define. For some reason, I could never really remember what it meant. But one day, we drove by a store called Serendipity, and Mom quickly pointed it out saying that if she ever started a business, she would call it Karendipity because that is how much she loved the word. At the time, I cringed, because I was not a fan of Mom's jokes, and today I cringe because of what we all think when we hear the name Karen (lol). Anyway, it wasn't until moments ago, scrolling through pictures of "tasteful tattoos," that serendipity ran across my screen, bringing with it a plethora of memories. And though it took years, I believe that I am now finally beginning to understand what serendipity means. Merriam-Webster defines serendipity as "the faculty or phenomenon of finding valuable or agreeable things not sought for." So, isn't grief serendipitous? Along with this book, our memories, our lives, and our deaths. Though these things bring sadness, they also show love and happiness. Even though the pain that arises from loss is immeasurable, so seems the happiness that we hold in our memories, and so seems the beauty that lies within the sadness that we feel because of unexpressed love.

For me, grief has been serendipitous. Through grief, I was able to realize my strength and learn that it is okay to be weak. Grief helped me understand empathy, and how to be a better friend to myself and others. Because of grief, I realized the love that I had for my parents, and the importance of expressing my love to the people around me. Grief showed me where I was being stubborn and what I needed to work on. Grief taught me that I can value something I hate, and that every last feeling I have is important. So, I guess I tend to find valuable or agreeable things not sought for in each moment of grief, no matter how much grief fucking sucks.

So, I guess that's my grief. And I guess that this is the end of this book. Hopefully, sharing my story has helped you to better understand your own, or it's given you something to take with you into the rest of your beautiful life.

All the love,
Taya

I miss you,
I love you,
and thank you.

CPSIA information can be obtained
at www.ICGtesting.com
Printed in the USA
LVHW072022120123
736980LV00018B/103

9 781039 138186